MRS
ZIGZAG

MRS ZIGZAG

THE EXTRAORDINARY LIFE OF A SECRET AGENT'S WIFE

BETTY CHAPMAN & RONALD L. BONEWITZ

The History Press

To Lilian Verner-Bonds, who encouraged the writing of this book.

All cover images courtesy of the Chapman collection.

First published 2013

The History Press
The Mill, Brimscombe Port
Stroud, Gloucestershire, GL5 2QG
www.thehistorypress.co.uk

British Library Cataloguing in Publication Data.
A catalogue record for this book is available from the British Library.

ISBN 978 0 7524 8813 4

Typesetting and origination by The History Press
Printed in Great Britain
Manufacturing managed by Jellyfish Solutions Ltd

CONTENTS

FOREWORD

BY NIGEL WEST

E arly in March 1980 I found myself in Claygate, south-west London, in the company of an elderly British army officer, Major Michael Ryde, who had fallen on hard times. I was meeting him because I had heard that during the war he had served in MI5 as a Regional Security Liaison Officer, the post held by the organisation's represent-atives who acted as an intermediary between the counter-espionage branch, designated B Division, and individual military district com-manders. Over a cup of coffee served by his long-suffering partner, Marjorie Caton-Jones, Ryde recalled his recruitment into the Security Service and happier times, when he routinely had been engaged in the most secret work, much of it involved in the handling of double agents. As he gained enthusiasm for his subject, and his improving memory allowed him to add the kind of detail that ensures authenticity, these revelations visibly moved Marjorie who confided to me later that in all the years she had lived with the veteran, he had never mentioned his wartime intelligence role. As a professional journalist of long standing, having worked on *The Sunday Telegraph* for years, she had developed a skill for listening, and on this occasion she sat rapt as the man she had known and lived with described a part of his life that hitherto had been entirely unknown to her. Later, she would reproach herself for having failed to apply her inquiring mind to the one man who had played such an important part in her recent life.

Major Ryde's story largely revolved around his relationship with a Nazi spy, code named Fritzchen, who had been expected to parachute into East Anglia towards the end of December 1942. Much was already known about him at MI5's headquarters in St James's Street, information that had been gleaned from ISK and ISOS, the cryptographic source based on intercepts of the *Abwehr*'s internal communications. The German training school in Nantes, where Fritzchen had been based, was connected to Berlin by a radio link as the occupiers learned to distrust the French landline telephone system. With regional operations supervised in every detail from the *Abwehr*'s main building on the Tirpitzufer, the airwaves were entrusted with the most banal details of the progress made by agents undergoing preparation for missions in enemy territory. Fritzchen was known to be a British renegade, paid a regular monthly salary of 450 Reichsmarks, with an agreed bonus of 100,000 Reichsmarks, then valued at £15,000, if he pulled off his sabotage assignment successfully. As well as mentioning his contractual arrangements, the intercepts listed the two aliases he would adopt in England, the frequencies of his wireless transmitter and the detail of his dental repairs.

In Fritzchen's case, his planned departure was delayed by a training accident when he had been injured while practising a parachute drop. After several false alarms, Ryde had been alerted to the imminent arrival of the much-anticipated spy on a clandestine Luftwaffe flight from Le Bourget in mid-December, and he finally landed near Ely on the night of 20 December, three days late. Ryde had been waiting patiently for this news, but he could not be certain of the exact location of the drop-zone, nor the likely attitude of the spy. Worst case, Fritzchen, who was known to have a criminal past, would prove to be intransigent and uncooperative, making MI5's task more complicated. On the other hand, he might be wholly willing to collaborate, and then there was always the middle path, of the spy conditioned to self-preservation, who would take on whatever guise that would save him from the gallows.

Ryde recalled the moment, in Littleport's tiny police station, that the Chief Constable of Cambridgeshire had ushered him into the interview room where he was confronted with Fritzchen, the first Nazi spy of his acquaintance, and who was equipped with £1,000 in notes, a loaded automatic and a suicide pill. This would be the beginning of an extraordinary adventure that would end in January 1946 when MI5 learned that the double agent known to them as Zigzag intended to disclose his remarkable story in the French newspaper *L'Etoile du Soir*. The result was a criminal prosecution at the Old Bailey on charges under the Official Secrets Act in an attempt to remind Zigzag, and other double agents also tempted to recount their experiences. MI5's leading lawyer, Edward Cussen KC, discussed the options at length with his Director of B Division, Guy Liddell, who confided to the diary he dictated every evening that authority had been given for Cussen to travel to Paris to investigate what was regarded as a significant breach of faith.

Cussen returned to London with the evidence required to arrest Zigzag, and it was intended that a private session in a magistrate's court, held in camera, with a stern lecture from the bench, would act as a deterrent, not just for Zigzag, but for any others interested in publishing indiscreet memoirs. However, MI5's intentions were thwarted when, to the surprise of the prosecuting counsel, the defence had called Major Michael Ryde, who had testified on oath at his trial at Bow Street Court on 19 March, without any approval from MI5, that the defendant was 'the bravest man he had ever met' and that, far from deserving to be in the dock, he should receive a medal. Thus ended Ryde's career in the Security Service, and gave Eddie Chapman the confidence to tell his truly incredible tale.

Thanks to Michael Ryde, and an introduction provided by him, I was soon sharing coffee with Eddie Chapman and his equally extraordinary wife, Betty, at their apartment in the Barbican. Always modest about his own exploits, the legendary double agent regarded his encounters with MI5 as only a small part of an extraordinary career. Fortunately, Betty knew better!

INTRODUCTION

I was introduced to Betty and Eddie Chapman several years before Eddie's passing in 1997, by Lilian Verner-Bonds, a mutual friend and a long-time friend of the Chapmans. One of my great regrets is that I didn't know more about Eddie at the time. Sketchy details of his past were known, but my recollection of that first meeting is of a pleasant, late-middle-age couple in their comfortable but far from extravagant surroundings. We shared a pleasant tea together, during which the conversation passed as nothing remarkable, leaving me with a recollection of a nice gentleman who said very little. As the years passed, so too Eddie passed away. I was encouraged over a long period to start writing the story of his wife Betty, which is equally remarkable. The time was never right, until now.

This book was constructed from numerous interviews, documents, Betty's notebooks spanning several decades, and from taped reminiscences of Betty and Eddie, which were generously provided by the Chapman family. Other information has come from documentary sources. In her nineties, Betty is still bright and lucid, with an excellent memory. Where possible, this story has been told in her own words: my role is principally that of narrator. Where Betty's language may, in a very few places, seem 'politically incorrect', it must be remembered that she is a woman of her generation: a woman of substance by dint of her own efforts, and a British woman living through the transition from British Empire to Commonwealth. I have never, through long interviews and in examining innumerable pages of her notes and writings, seen the faintest hint of prejudice. This is especially true as she describes her adventures in Africa and the Middle East. She simply reports what she has seen and done, and takes all who she met as they are, on their own merits.

It may also be asked as to why she didn't have more detailed knowledge of some of Eddie's post-war activities. There are several answers to this. First, although Eddie was a consummate storyteller – often not bothering too much with accuracy – he was careful about *what* he told. He survived as a double agent by knowing when to keep his mouth closed. As, indeed, he did when I first met him. While he might weave fascinating tales about his adventures, there were many things about which he had nothing to say – especially in the presence of Betty. This is the second point: Eddie was always very protective of his wife, and never would have put her at risk by telling her too much. It is also important to remember that in British society of the time, even into the latter half of the twentieth century, it was not unusual for a wife not to know her husband's income – or for that matter even what he did for a living. In this context it is not surprising that Eddie's activities when he was away from Betty still are not fully known to her. There is no doubt that she was his anchor and he wanted her involved in many of his ventures – and to be involved in hers. But this was far from the sum and total of Eddie's life, or Betty's.

Eddie Chapman was a man as complex as the space shuttle, but with many components that worked in direct opposition to each other. How it must have been to have lived with such a man is difficult to imagine. Who could have imagined that this young farm girl from the back of beyond would become the honoured guest of Middle Eastern royal families, the confidante and hostess of an African president, the friend of film stars? Yet Betty Chapman, née Farmer, not only grew as a person while with this man, but in her later years when I met her turned out to be a delightful and thoroughly charming lady, whereas other women under the same circumstances might have grown dark and embittered.

Many readers will ask themselves as they progress through the book: 'Why on Earth did she stay with him?' The answer is as complicated as their relationship. Because both Eddie and Betty were extraordinary people in their own right, their relationship cannot be judged by the standards of 'normal' relationships. Eddie was more like a force of nature: the torrent of water flowing around the rock that was Betty – each in their own roles.

The counsellor and therapist Lilian Verner-Bonds, a long-time friend of the Chapmans, adds: 'Betty was never Eddie's victim. She had the same strength and steel as he did. That is why they were perfectly suited, and she was able to give him the support she did. They were two peas in a pod.'

Some readers may be tempted to make judgements about Eddie Chapman based on Betty's experiences related in this book. My advice is: don't. There is no doubt that Eddie was a difficult man, but from everything I know about him, and from the brief time I spent with him and Betty before his passing, he was not a *bad* man. Indeed, there will be more than one reader of this book who is alive today because of him, and at considerable risk to his own life. The total number is likely to run into thousands.

Betty herself is a deeply spiritual woman, and has always had the feeling that no matter how it came about and whatever experiences resulted, she and Eddie were *meant* to be together. This has been emphasised to me time and again by Betty during the preparation of this book, and I have not the slightest inclination to dispute it. She views their life together as their mutual karma. Karma has many definitions, but the only one that really matters for Betty is this: 'I just felt like his life was his karma, so my life was my karma. Your karma means that it's what was meant to be, what you were fated to do. Because if you believe that you have lived before, this is the continuation. This is something you've come back to do, whether it's pleasant or unpleasant.'

One of Eddie's biographers went to the heart of the matter: 'How Eddie and Betty got together is one of the more implausible stories in a lifetime of unlikely happenings. That she stayed with him – as Eddie faced up to his demons – is the most extraordinary thing of all.'

It is hoped that this book will shed light on that very thing.

Dr Ronald Bonewitz
Rogate, England, 2013

PROLOGUE:
AGENT ZIGZAG

Zigzag was the name given by British Intelligence to one of the most audacious double agents of the Second World War – Arnold Edward 'Eddie' Chapman.

Eddie had been born in Sunderland to a middle-class professional family but his father, a marine engineer, had spent most of Eddie's childhood away at sea, and his mother had struggled to bring up her two boys more or less alone. When Eddie was young, he was an apprentice in the shipping industry with Thompson's shipbuilders. Whilst he was there he saved a young man from drowning. Yet when he was interviewed about the incident he denied having saved the man, as he thought his mother would beat him for not being at school. Later he was given a medal for that act of bravery.

Eddie grew restless, bought an old bicycle and rode the 200 or so miles to London. He lied about his age and enlisted in the military – the elite Coldstream Guards, one of the most prestigious regiments in the British Army. In one of history's great ironies, he wound up at the Tower of London, guarding the Crown Jewels. Within a short time he had absconded from the military and taken up a new career – as a safe-cracker. He and his gang were successful enough at their new enterprise that Scotland Yard set up a special task force just to track them down.

In 1939 Eddie went to the island of Jersey with his girlfriend, Betty Farmer, intending to go on to France to escape the authorities. Here, the police caught up with him. He was arrested and sentenced to a jail term in Jersey. While he was incarcerated, the Second World War broke out, and Jersey was occupied by the Germans. He offered his services to Nazi Germany as a spy and a traitor, whilst intending all along to become a British double agent. Germany eventually accepted his offer. He was given the name Fritz Graumann (to the Germans Agent Fritzchen) and was trained by the *Abwehr* (a German spy network) in explosives, radio communications, parachute jumping and other subjects, before being dispatched to England in 1942 to commit acts of sabotage. He immediately surrendered himself to the police before offering his services to British Intelligence, MI5. Thanks to top-secret Ultra intercepts, MI5 had prior knowledge of Agent Fritzchen's mission, which corresponded in every aspect with the story Eddie told them. Convinced he was genuine in his offer to be a double agent, MI5 decided to use him. MI5 faked a sabotage attack on his target, the de Havilland aircraft factory in Hatfield, Hertfordshire, where the Mosquito bomber was being manufactured.

Now acting for the British as Zigzag – a code name assigned to him by MI5 – he made his way back to his German controllers in occupied France (after being questioned by the Gestapo), and was awarded the Iron Cross for his work as a saboteur. He was then sent to Norway to teach at a German spy school in Oslo. Immediately after D-Day he was sent back to Britain to report on the accuracy of the V-1 weapon, which was just being launched against London. Back in contact with MI5, he passed on information about the Germans that he had gathered at great personal risk in Oslo. He also consistently reported to the Germans that the bombs were overshooting their central London target, when in fact they were regularly landing in the city. The Germans corrected their aim, with the end result that many bombs fell short in the Kent countryside, doing far less damage than they otherwise would have done, and saving a great many lives.

Eddie was reunited with Betty in 1945, and they eventually married in 1947. After the war, Chapman remained friends with Baron von Gröning, his *Abwehr* handler, who was a thoroughly decent man, and who was later guest of honour at the wedding of Betty and Eddie's daughter.

Fanny Johnstone of *The Guardian* newspaper wrote in 2007:

> Spies have always been romantic figures, and the idea of having a love affair, or even a marriage, with one, has inspired a host of stories and characters ... But these stories rarely tell us much about what it's really like ... a life we assume to be glamorous, and know to be precarious, but which has never been accurately described.[1]

Perhaps this book goes some way to describe the experience, for the wife of one spy, at least.

1

EDDIE IS DEAD, LONG LIVE EDDIE

The February sun was unusually dazzling as it shone through the French windows of the restaurant, sending up sparkles from the fine crystal and polished silver adorning the elegant tablecloth. Equally dazzling was the blonde woman sitting with three male companions. They had let it be known that they were 'film people' and it took no imagination whatsoever to believe that the Harlowesque blonde was the star of some upcoming celluloid epic. The man to whom she devoted most of her attention was film–star material himself – tall, thin, rakishly handsome and with a thin moustache. The two rougher men with them easily could have been mistaken for bodyguards. The woman was Betty Farmer, and they had been in Jersey for a week. This lazy, idyllic Sunday lunchtime in February 1939 was among the best moments of her life. She couldn't have imagined that she was just a few heartbeats away from the worst.

The handsome man was talking to her about a boat trip that he had seen advertised in the harbour area, but she recalls that her attention was more taken by the small vase of freesias that smelt 'absolutely heavenly'. At some stage in the conversation, however, she became aware that both the tone and the speed of his speech had changed. Before she knew what was happening, he leapt from his seat, kissed her shoulder and dived through the closed French windows in a shower of broken glass. The man now disappearing through the gardens of the hotel, leaving behind shattered glass, broken crockery, shouting waiters and policemen, and a bewildered and stunned Betty, was Arnold Edward Chapman – professional criminal, safe-breaker extraordinaire, and wanted man. The next time he and Betty would meet, nearly six years later, he would be Arnold Edward Chapman, darling of both the German and British intelligence services, one of the most audacious double agents of all time, and loose cannon. And, grudgingly – to the British Establishment at least – a national hero: Agent Zigzag.

Those few minutes of utter chaos in the restaurant were, unbeknown to Betty Farmer, the pivot point of her life.

Born twenty-two years previously on a small farm near Neen Sollars in Shropshire, Betty was the first of eleven children. If there was a far corner of the Earth in the late 1930s, the farms surrounding this minuscule village in the English midlands were it. The village comprised a few houses, a public house, a church and a school. Betty's nearest neighbour was a mile away. The farm was surrounded by woodlands and she had to walk to and from her house along a small track a mile or so long, which led to a narrow tarmac road. She walked everywhere, except when the weather was very bad and her father took her in his pony carriage. They would drive some 3 or 4 miles to a main road, and then she walked the rest of the way to school. It was miles away, quite literally, from the bright lights of London and the glittering, glamorous life that awaited her.

As a teenager Betty's emerging beauty hadn't gone unnoticed. For a time she went out with the son of the local squire. She was very keen on him but he finally finished the relationship to go out with a more sophisticated girl who had come to the area from London. Betty had a further complication in that the local vicar had fallen in love with her.[1] She was going out with him at the same time that she was dating the squire's son. When that relationship finished she was very upset, but did not want to continue her relationship with the vicar. This caused a local scandal in the village:

People thought I was flighty and as I did not intend to have a serious relationship with the vicar I decided the easiest option was to leave. To be honest, I did not want the responsibility of bringing up my 10 brothers and sisters either, so that was a part of my decision to leave, but not the main reason. So, I decided to go to London.

It is hard to imagine in the twenty-first century how radical such a step was. Even as late as the 1960s it was difficult for a single woman to get a bank account in England without a man's signature. Dickensian England did not die with Charles Dickens.

Of that time, Betty recalls:

My mother was a very good mother. She worked hard bringing up eleven children with only her mother's help to aid her. She did all the cooking and baking, and father was always out working, running the farm. They were very upset when I left; they did not want me to leave and I didn't see my mother and father for a good many years afterwards. But I wanted a fresh start and London was a big city with lots of opportunities. The situation at home with Richard and the vicar was too awkward so I needed to leave. I had a few hundred pounds, which was given to me by my two aunts who lived in Rhyl, and who wanted to help me. I used to go to them when I needed clothes and money and they would help me out. My aunts were on my mother's side of the family. They spent their life in service working for the same family, who were very wealthy. When the last of the family died they did not have any heirs, so left their estate to my aunts. I had the name of an Irish lady, Wonnie Carey, who ran a bed-and-breakfast boarding house for young ladies in Baron's Court, west London. I moved in and she took me under her wing.

Wonnie Carey introduced Betty to many people, including Charles Hawtree who owned hotels on the Isle of Man, where she later trained for a year to learn the hotel business.

Because I had been brought up very religiously, I carried on going to church. Wonnie would go to church but she was Catholic. Whenever I've been in different countries, whatever the faith, I've always gone to church. I used to go with her to the Catholic Church. There were two rules: no trousers, and you had to wear gloves on Sunday.

Betty also adds with a chuckle: 'no smoking or swearing or any of that either! She was a very religious lady and ran what was referred to at the time as a good clean house. I met a lot of people through her. She was very "correct".' Betty chuckles again: 'I couldn't have a fellow in. The telephone was in the hallway and if you were expecting a call you hung around in the hallway. There wasn't much privacy.'

Young, pretty and vivacious, Betty went out from time to time with a man she met at the B&B who took her out to a number of London clubs. It was during this time that she was offered the job of social secretary at a social club on Church Street in Kensington (a wealthy enclave of London) as an evening job. She also worked in a fashion shop during the day. It was at this club that she had her first encounter with Eddie Chapman. One evening as she was playing on the pinball machine a member came in with a new young man. The new man, tall, thin and handsome, stood by the machine having a drink with his friend, and as she moved away, she heard the newcomer say 'I'm going to marry her.'

'In a pig's ear!' she replied.

Despite her 'pig's ear' remark, she ended up talking with him and having a drink. He said he wanted to see her again. He told her that at that time he was sharing a cottage in Hertfordshire with Terence Young. Young was best known in later years for directing three of the films in the James Bond series, *Dr No*, *From Russia with Love* and *Thunderball*. In his Wikipedia profile, it says: 'Terence Young WAS James Bond'. There is little doubt that Young fitted the profile of Bond – the erudite, sophisticated ladykiller, dressed in Savile Row suits, always witty, well-versed in wine, and comfortable at home and abroad. It was remarked that Sean Connery, the first Bond, 'was simply doing a Terence Young impression'. It doesn't require too much imagination to believe that so, too, was Eddie. Terence was already flirting with the film business by then, so later when Eddie accounted to Betty for his absences as being related to films, it was entirely credible. That he was involved with a criminal gang and out blowing safes would never have entered Betty's mind.

Despite Betty's initial resistance, they started going out together. Gradually, a romance developed and, in late 1938, they began living together. Betty continues: 'In those days, living together was frowned upon by everyone: by one's parents, by the Church and, if one were in normal employment, by one's employers.' As a safebreaker, however, the normal conditions of employment were a little different for Eddie and, even if he had not been handsome and captivatingly charming, she would still have found the excitement of being with him to have been 'almost unbearable'. It is also worth remembering that Betty still believed that Eddie was 'in films', and as such the 'normal conditions of employment' didn't apply there either. At one point, Eddie revealed to Terence that he was, in fact, a crook and blew up safes for a living. Far from being shocked, Terence saw this as adding to the excitement and glamour of their lives.

It *was* a glamorous time, even though the clubs Eddie took Betty to were on the sleazy side. But as she remarks: 'they were places of their time'. Eddie himself was a glamorous character, and seemed to know all of the club owners, although why he should was a mystery to Betty. In reality, Eddie moved in the criminal underworld; the clubs he took Betty to were his natural haunts. By the time Betty went to Jersey, she knew this.

Betty takes up the story of the startling events on Jersey, with her and Eddie checked into a hotel as 'Mr and Mrs Farmer' of Torquay:

The restaurant at the Hotel de la Plage, right on the waterfront in Havre des Pas, was *the* place in Jersey to eat. I loved it. Restaurants in London were, at this time, normally more hushed and a little stuffy but here, in Jersey, the atmosphere was alive with a buzz of conversation that belied the awful events unfolding across Europe. The decor was distinctly European, the walls were painted a creamy lemon, the colour of syllabub, the tablecloths were crisp, white linen and the menus were handwritten on sheets of cream vellum. There was a loud woman with a ridiculous hat and a tired fox fur sitting at the table next to ours. She'd talked incessantly since she had sat down but, as she spoke in French and as her clothes were different and more stylish than those I was used to, I really didn't mind. I was 22 years old and in love with the most handsome and charismatic man I had ever seen and I couldn't remember ever having been happier.

We had been living together for a little over three months – three months of electric excitement for me and three months of evading the law for Eddie. As I had only recently discovered, in those three months, and for many months before, he and his group of friends had carried out a number of audacious safebreakings in London and things had become more than a little difficult, with an unprecedented amount of interest on the part of the Metropolitan Police – the Met.

In the spring of 1938, the Met set up a special squad to hunt him down. Eddie was far from hiding out – he was out nightclubbing with Betty or travelling down to the seaside resort of Brighton to spend the loot. Nevertheless, he had decided that his run of luck was wearing a bit thin – like all career criminals – so he decided to stop breaking safes for 'a whole year'. His 'retirement' lasted less than six weeks. With a sort of sixth sense that the police were closing in, Eddie decided to make his way to Jersey, and from there on to France.

Betty continues:

In an attempt to lie low for a while and to allow the heat to subside, we had come to Jersey to take advantage of the early spring, and the holiday atmosphere that was so different from the relentless worry and anticipation of pre-war London. Even though I was happy in that moment in the bright sunshine, nonetheless for the last three months I had lain awake in the small hours of countless mornings, wondering how I might continue if Eddie were to be caught and wondering what would become of us if that were to happen. On Jersey, we had a lovely holiday; we danced on the beach and I'd enjoyed Eddie's wonderful sense of humour.

After Eddie had disappeared through the window, other policemen immediately took charge of Eddie's two 'friends', who had lacked the presence of mind to follow Eddie through the window. Later identified as members of his criminal gang, they were handcuffed and taken away. As normal conversation returned to the restaurant – at least as normal as was possible after the startling events of the past few minutes – Betty sat frozen to the spot. The awful truth was dawning on her that she was a girl not long out of her teens, all alone in what was to all intents and purposes a foreign land. She had very little money, as Eddie always paid for everything, and she had absolutely no idea how to find her way home. That night, alone in her hotel room, she resolved to stay in Jersey until she could find out what had happened to Eddie. The Jersey police had other ideas.

The following morning, her plans were rudely interrupted by a visit from the police, who wanted to know the extent to which she could help them and their Met colleagues from London to piece together the details of a string of robberies. Until now these crimes had defied attempts by a number of police forces to solve them. Betty recalls:

> I was taken to the police station and I sat there in abject misery, not knowing what to say and fearing that anything I might say might further incriminate Eddie. Worst of all, it appeared that he might be returned to London to stand trial and I was terrified that all the robberies with which he had been involved, and many others with which he had not, would all be pinned on him in court and that it might be many years before I would see him again. Even though I already knew that Eddie was a criminal and wanted man, I still felt that he had let me down and I was hurt and upset.

Even while Betty sat in the police station, Eddie was still on the run in Jersey. Back in London, a couple of weeks earlier, he had been told that the police were looking for him. 'A man I knew said that if we could reach Monte Carlo,' Eddie later remembered, 'he could get us on a boat for South America.' He decided he could fly to Jersey, just a few miles off the French coast, and then make his way south to Monte Carlo. He had decided to take Betty with him. Once through the window, and despite being recognised and nearly apprehended by the police, he still believed he had a chance to escape.

After his dramatic exit, he found a place to temporarily hide out in an unoccupied school. He found an old mackintosh to cover his distinctive and colourful clothing – yellow-spotted tie, blue sleeveless pullover, grey flannels, brown sandals and no socks – and eventually made his way to a seedy boarding house, run by a suspicious landlady. He told her he was a marine engineer, but when his picture – to his consternation – was splashed over the front page of the newspaper the next day, the landlady called the police. She reported that her lodger fitted the description of the escaped criminal.

The police told the local populace that caution should be exercised in his apprehension, because he was, they claimed, 'dangerous' – despite never having used violence, or even (his specialty was burglary) encountered another person in the course of his 'activities'. Eddie was away from the boarding house at the time the police were called. Having had the shock of seeing his picture all over the newspapers, he realised the game was up. So, in typical Eddie Chapman style, he decided to go out with a splash. Arriving at a nightclub – presumably after ditching the grubby mackintosh – he ordered champagne. Also in typical Chapman style, he slipped down to the basement and broke into the club's safe in order to pay for it. Arriving back at the boarding house at 2 a.m., he was immediately arrested, the landlady having phoned the police to report his return.

Betty was all over the papers as well. The *Jersey Evening Post* reported the next day: 'She is stated to have denied all knowledge of the alleged activities of her companions.' Although the Jersey papers were full of the story, they were sympathetic to her plight. The tone of the stories was that she was an unwitting victim of the situation, which was true enough in many respects. She had committed no crime and hadn't been an accomplice to any crimes. As Eddie had made it perfectly clear to the authorities upon his arrest, Betty knew nothing about his activities or why they were on the island, other than for a holiday. But suddenly she was alone in Jersey, 'I didn't know what to do, I was in shock. The people of Jersey rallied around and came to my rescue, collecting enough cash to get me back to London. Eddie was in custody, and there was nothing more I could do'. Eddie was being held in Jersey, and because his last crime was committed in Jersey, he was to be jailed there. Little was she to know that even though he was to be held in St Helier, it would still be nearly six years before they would be together once more.

With Eddie incarcerated and incommunicado, the shocked Betty returned to London to decide what to do next. Still very young, she had no real training or skills, except, inadvertently, evading the law.

When I got back to London, there was the question of 'now what?' I contacted Charles Hawtree, to whom I had previously been introduced, and was offered the opportunity to go to the Isle of Man to learn the hotel trade in one of his hotels. Meanwhile, my family had heard about the goings-on in Jersey. None of them thought I should be mixing with someone who was a criminal and they considered him to be not good enough for me. Other friends thought I ought to try to get in touch with him but although I attempted to contact him I was not able to. It wasn't too long after this that the war broke out, and the Germans invaded Jersey. I remember wondering what we all would do and where we would go and what would happen to us. And that was the end of any attempt to either contact Eddie or, for that matter, even find out what had become of him. Of course, he managed to get in with the Germans once they arrived and occupied the island, and he had this notion of offering to work for them. I didn't know anything about this at the time.

Finally, word got back to Betty that the Germans had executed Eddie. A German newspaper clipping of the time shows a man identified as Eddie tied to a stake ready to be shot. This was part of the German cover story as they turned Eddie into 'Agent Fritzchen'. A close examination of the man in the photo reveals that he bears only superficial resemblance to Eddie. Who this unfortunate was, and whether the picture is of a genuine execution, is unknown. Little did Betty know, or could even have imagined, what was really happening …

SPITFIRES, SABOTAGE AND SERIAL KILLERS

On 1 July 1940, German troops poured into Jersey, where Eddie was still in jail. The island was essentially undefended, and within a few weeks life settled into a routine for both the islanders and their occupiers. For the most part, in the early days the Germans were on their best behaviour. Little changed for Eddie and his fellow prisoners. Surprisingly, perhaps, the Germans honoured the decision of the courts made prior to the invasion and, with some delay, Eddie was released from prison at the beginning of October 1941. There was no chance of communicating with the outside world, and thus Betty had no idea that he was still alive.

But what was alive and well was Eddie's fertile mind. He soon was involved in black market activities – with the tacit approval of the Germans. Shortly after his release he also contacted the German commander and offered his 'services', citing his hatred of the English and a desire for revenge. Despite this being a clever ploy to get off the island, the Germans apparently took his offer at face value. But by November Eddie was in trouble with the authorities – apparently. He was arrested for sabotage and sent to the French mainland. He was never certain, but it always appeared to him that it was a ruse to get him out of Jersey and into the hands of German Intelligence.

Once in France, Eddie was incarcerated in the prison at Romainville, where he seemed to be in some danger of being shot. Even so, Eddie had been very inventive whilst in prison and had actually managed to copy keys to the neighbouring ladies' prison, and indeed spent many very pleasant nights with them. All of this changed abruptly in April 1942, when he was released into the custody of German Intelligence and began a reasonably comfortable period being trained as a German spy. Although watched closely, he maintained his all too believable story of having a grudge against the English. In the meantime, his training in sabotage, communications, and other skills necessary for the role of a spy and saboteur continued.

At the same time, Betty, believing him dead, was on the Isle of Man learning all she could about the hotel business, which she loved. Betty remarks: 'it served me in good stead for what my life was to become'. Indeed it did. She was later to start the first (and hugely successful) health farm in Britain, and came to own a castle in Ireland, among her numerous other ventures.

I went to the Isle of Man, and I had the marvellous romance in some ways on the Isle of Man. He was a brigadier and in those days he was a big shot and he was just nuts about me. We used to have such fun, and get up to lots of tricks. For a brigadier, to me he wasn't that old and the man who owned the hotel was also keen about me, so it was very awkward to keep those two apart.

I loved sport; that is to say, I always loved the sport in which my current love was involved. The Isle of Man was quite an exciting thing in a way because of the TT racing[1] and we also used to go horse riding. I was out riding one morning on top of a hill with an elderly character called Sandy Powell. He just went 'titch, titch' and my horse bolted. Watching was a famous ladies' band leader called Ivy Benson, and she later remarked that I looked like the man on the flying trapeze. I thought, 'my god if it goes left it will go into the sea off a high cliff', and there was also an electric railway that went through the centre of the island. Well, fortunately it turned right and went back to the stables, but meanwhile it had thrown me and was dragging me by my ankle. Fortunately someone stopped it, but by then my ankle was broken. I felt I was lucky just to get away with no more than that.

Unlike the Nazis who believed that women should stay home to produce the next generation of German soldiers, Britain went on a 'total war' footing almost from the start. When Betty returned to London – just in time for the Blitz – she immediately went into war work. During the war, London buzzed with the energy of soldiers, sailors and airmen of many nations living life to the full while they still could. Now back in London, Betty was part of this frantic whirl, and was drawn into the glamorous and exciting world of aviators and test pilots. Still unaware that Eddie was alive, she had fallen madly in love with a man who she charmingly describes as 'a Spitfire pilot', Peter Powell. He was, in fact, a great deal more than 'a Spitfire pilot'. For more than a year before the United States entered the Second World War some of its young men went through Canada to enlist in the Royal Air Force (RAF) to fight Germany alongside the British – in violation of the American neutrality acts. Initially somewhat disorganised, eventually in 1941 the British decided to organise three squadrons of Americans, the so-called Eagle Squadrons. One of these was the legendary 121 Squadron, and its first commander was Squadron Leader Peter Powell.
Betty recalls:

I met Peter Powell in a pub in Mayfair where military and air force people met.[2] I thought he was a nice young man and I was attracted to him at once. I did not realise how famous he was when I met him but soon found out. We met regularly; he visited me in London and took me out to pubs and to meet his friends. Ben Bowrings was a friend of mine and Peter's who also flew Spitfires. His wife Zena and I would count them coming back after a raid and if one was missing we were in a state until we knew they were both okay. We would meet at a local (pub) after a sortie and it was often a meeting of relief and sadness: relief at having Ben and Peter with us, but sorrow if one of the boys was missing. I can still remember the highs and lows of those days.

As all of this was taking place, Eddie was undergoing espionage and sabotage training in France. After the war, Betty learned about Eddie's exploits while he was in France, and takes up the story:

When Eddie was training to be a spy in the *Dienststelle* (*WASt*), he had a caretaker, a friend, whose name was Tomas. He was German but had been partly educated in England. Although Eddie spoke German before going there, he had to perfect it. Eddie enjoyed his training, he thought a lot of it was fun, highly dangerous but fun – but Eddie loved anything that was dangerous! He described Morse code as 'black art'. After the war we received a case of wine from Tomas, out of the blue, when we were living at Shenley Lodge. That was a nice thought. On one occasion Eddie got bored during his training and he took off alone, which was forbidden. He went to a local bordello, where he met a girl and he spent the day with her. When Baron von Gröning (Eddie's commanding officer and overseer of the *Dienststelle,* later a life-long friend of the Chapmans) found out he was missing, he was disturbed; he was always worried about Eddie anyway, taking a special interest in him – and never being totally certain whether Eddie was a British agent or not. He sent out three members from the *Dienststelle* to find him, which they did, and Eddie invited them to have a drink with him! The upshot was that they all returned legless. They had ordered two bottles of cognac and a bottle of liquor! One by one they were very sick. Von Gröning was happy with the outcome: they got back safely but were punished with a giant hangover.

Among the other things that Eddie got up to during his training was that he would go into the dining room in the morning, go up to the portrait of Hitler and shake his fists at it rather than raising his arm in salute. For some reason, the Germans thought this was hilarious. Only Eddie could have got away with it.

After a long period of training, the day came for him to put his training into practice. Eddie was parachuted into Cambridgeshire in eastern England at 2 a.m. on 20 December 1942. He knocked on the front door of a nearby farmhouse to say that he was an airman who had just landed and needed help. The farmer then got in touch with the police. Eddie was picked up and immediately asked to be put in touch with British Intelligence. He was handed over to them at Latchmere House, Ham Common, where they kept espionage suspects. Terence Young was recalled from the Middle East to identify him. Soon after, British Intelligence interviewed Eddie and he told them everything, just as he had planned to. Finally, after much interrogation and doubts on the part of his interrogators, they came to an agreement that he would be of use to them. He was accepted by the Double Cross Committee under the command of John C. Masterman, as a double agent.

Eddie's mission for the Germans was to blow up the de Havilland factory in Hertfordshire, where the Mosquito bomber had been built. He divulged all of this in full to his MI5 interrogators.[3] An illusionist called Jasper Maskelyne was called in to make the factory look as though it had been sabotaged, and a German reconnaissance aircraft was allowed through to take pictures of the 'damage'.[4] Even the local British civilians believed that the site had been bombed; it was even in the newspaper. This fake sabotage was carried out on 29 January. Eddie's 'destruction' of the factory was so elaborately faked that the Germans were completely taken in. Before returning to France with the blessing of British Intelligence to continue his espionage activities against the Nazis, it is quite likely that he and Betty passed within a short distance of each other in London. It is probably just as well that they did not meet at that point in time, as it would have compromised Eddie's position as a double agent, an increasingly valuable one as the war progressed.

At the same time as Eddie's intelligence activities were taking place, Betty was busily involved in the war effort, driving an ambulance and working in a factory making war materials – small parts for aircraft:

'It was during the war and everyone was supposed to work to further the war effort so I got allocated the job. I was the inspector at the end of the bench. Everyone was working too hard and the atmosphere was very competitive with everyone trying to do more than the next person.'

This was far from the end of Betty's input into the war effort:

At night I used to go up on the roof with all the soldiers and put out the fires started by incendiary bombs on the roof with buckets of water. I was very scared but as it always happened very quickly there was never time to worry about it. You just had to get on with it. There were explosive bombs falling around but they were never near enough to us to cause us harm. There were boys and men there helping, but they had to do the heavy manual work of carrying buckets of water up the stairs or ladders and pass them up to us on the roof.

As dangerous as this was, Betty had an even closer call:

I was on the way home in a taxi when the bombs started falling. I jumped out of the taxi and ended up flat on the ground on my knees as the bombs were exploding around me. The taxi driver had meanwhile done a runner and was nowhere to be seen.

Among the prestigious and attractive aviators she met during the war was Geoffrey de Havilland, Jr., son of the famous aircraft designer and English pioneer aviator of the same name. They were soon going out together. Betty recalls an event that might have been a practical joke … but may not have been. 'Somebody bought a box of kippers and let them go bad. Then he (or possibly she) posted them to Geoffrey. Those things today wouldn't be funny.' He became de Havilland's chief test pilot and made the maiden flights of both the 'wooden wonder' Mosquito and the jet-propelled Vampire. The film *The Sound Barrier* was based on the incident described by Betty in Chapter 3. Ironically, it was the de Havilland factory that Eddie was parachuted into by the Germans to blow up in 1942. Betty also knew the famous night-fighter pilot John Cunningham, dubbed 'Cat's Eyes Cunningham' by the press.[5] Yet Betty knew that Cunningham hated that name: it was just wartime propaganda.

It was around this same time that she met a casting director who became infatuated with her and wanted to launch her into films – another irony of Betty's life, since she and Eddie had represented themselves as 'film people' at the time of his arrest in Jersey. She appeared in a few films in small parts: with Sir Laurence Olivier in a tram scene; as a nun in *Come Us This Day*, with Valerie Hobson; as a land girl in some of the comedy films made at Riverside Studios. She soon realised that her future did not lie in that direction but, as she remarked, 'It was all money.'

One night during the war Betty was asked to go out with friends to a cocktail bar. One of them was Major Billy Moss, who wrote *Ili Met by Moonlight*:[6]

They said afterwards we were going for dinner with some friends so I should be prepared. We went to a club called the Spiders' Web on the Kingston bypass. It was a very nice place with a cabaret. When we got there who should be there but the young Duke of Kent, who was then 18. He was a friend of my friends and we were there to celebrate his 18th birthday. A friend of his mother, a countess, came along to see that we all behaved ourselves. One thing I remember very clearly was when the cabaret came on and the young duke was trying to be someone special, someone asked him what he thought of the cabaret and he said 'fucking awful'. I said that was the first time I had heard a duke swear! All in all, it was a lovely evening out.

Reflecting on her love life during that time, she reminisces:

When it came to romance I was definitely born under an unlucky star. I loved and lost so often. I either found the ones who were unavailable but desirable, or available but undesirable. I was fortunate not to lose my life to two well-known murderers. One was Colonel Jimmy Armstrong, whose real name was Neville Heath, and the other was John George Haigh, the 'acid bath killer' (see Chapter 3).

In March 1943 Eddie went back to France via Portugal, with instructions from the Germans to blow up the ship that transported him, via a bomb concealed in a lump of coal. This he reported to the ship's captain, who was aware of Eddie's identity. The bomb was later disposed of safely. He stayed in Portugal for some time and was interrogated by the Gestapo. Maintaining that he had important information about the British, he insisted that he would only pass it to von Gröning, who was by now on the Russian front. Eddie was adamant, and eventually von Gröning was recalled. In later years, von Gröning always asserted that his recall from Russia saved his life. It was probably true. The Germans awarded Eddie the Iron Cross for 'blowing up' the de Havilland factory.

Eddie was eventually sent on to Oslo, Norway. While there he had a romance with a local beauty who, it eventually transpired, was herself an intelligence officer working against the Nazis. Many idyllic months passed, with Eddie sailing with his new girlfriend, doing relatively little for the Germans – a bit of retraining in Morse – and a great deal of highly risky intelligence gathering for the British. Making the sort of promises to each other that people in wartime often do, he was parted from his lover and sent to Berlin. He would never see her again.

At a high-level meeting in Berlin on the eve of the D-Day landings (June 1944), it was decided that Eddie must parachute into England again, which was thought safer than arriving by boat, once again to land near Cambridge. This meeting was at such a high level, and was so secret, that the doors were locked and strict instructions given that they should not be disturbed. Senior officers of all the military forces were present, and the meeting went on through the night. When they emerged from the room messengers were waiting outside, having been denied access, and relayed the information that the Allied invasion had begun.

The Germans were about to launch their missile assault on London. A few days after D-Day, the Germans began launching their pilotless flying bombs, the V-1s, at London.[7] Eddie was to supply the Nazis with information about the fall of their V-1s. Along with another agent, he gave the Germans false information to suggest that the missiles were overshooting their target, thus leading the Germans to shorten their range and, as a result, dropping many of the bombs harmlessly in the farmlands short of London. It was arguably Eddie's most important contribution to the war effort, one that undoubtedly saved a great many civilian lives. But it was also the same parachute landing that damaged Eddie's back, and left him with a lifetime of pain. Furthermore, it led him indirectly into the Profumo Affair two decades later (see Chapter 7).

Ironically, Betty lost two homes to the very V-1s that Eddie was trying to divert. She recalls:

The first home I lost was when I was living out in the country, renting a cottage in Hampshire, near Fleet. Actually the cottage I had rented was near a field where they were building tank traps. That's where I had a little dog, a spaniel called Spitfire. He used to like male company and so he always used to visit the tank traps; the soldiers used to bring him back and they knew that they'd get a cup of tea.

The fact that the soldiers were able to sit and have a chat with a beautiful, upmarket blonde seems to have escaped her innocent recollection. She continues:

One day I was supposed to go to London but I didn't want to take Spitfire and I just couldn't leave him alone. The house in London I was heading off to was my previous address where I had to collect something. But in the end, I didn't go. That night the whole of the house was flattened by a buzz bomb. I would have been there should I have gone like I needed to. That house was at 28 Nevern Square in Earls Court.[8] That particular square was where I had earlier done my fire watching. Firefighting was hazardous. There were always fire-fighters on the go. Over a period the chances of getting killed were pretty good, because there were so many incendiaries. A bit later I moved into number 48 Nevern Square and I was visiting with a friend in nearby Gloucester Road when a buzz bomb passed near us and exploded. I joked that it couldn't possibly be my new home – and it was!! So in a short space of time I had lost two homes in the same square. Both those houses belonged to the same man. That day, the only person in the house was the housekeeper who got buried under all the rubble for eight hours, but fortunately she survived. Duncan Sandy, the son-in-law of Winston Churchill, announced too soon that the V-1s and V-2s had been crushed, and so masses of people who had evacuated came back to London. This infuriated Eddie as he was given information that there were more waves of V-1s and V-2s coming, he was very cross with him.

Betty had another near miss around that time – this time with a serial killer. It came about because of her friendship with another famous wartime pilot, Geoffrey Page, who had been shot down and badly burned. He was being treated by the famous Sir Archibald McIndoe, with whom Betty had become acquainted.[9] He, in turn, introduced her to 'Colonel Armstrong' (the alias of Neville Heath), who was supposed to be an officer from the Fleet Air Arm. His story was that he was flying airplanes from South Africa to London, that he was married, and that his wife had been killed while taking him to the airport in Johannesburg. With a shudder, Betty relates:

He proposed to me and said that I could be a mother to his child. When I went out with him he used to take me to the Eight Bells in Chelsea. He always wanted to come into my flat and have a good-night drink but something stopped me from ever allowing him up. One night he came to meet me with his fingers strapped up and I asked what happened. He told me he'd got into a fight the previous night with some Americans. I soon discovered that the night before in Notting Hill (west London) he had bitten off the breasts of a girl, and impaled her on a riding crop. His fingers had been injured in the struggle with her as she fought for her life. A policeman friend of mine later told me about this. By the time I had found out, he had left for Bournemouth, on the south coast. He'd asked me to go with him, but I wouldn't go. In Bournemouth, he met up with several Wrens, women from the military, and he murdered another woman. I was terrified because I thought: 'He is at large and loose and might come looking for me.' You think, 'Suppose he comes and I can't get

rid of him? If I can't hide I could probably end up the same way.'
Anyhow, he was found eventually.

Heath was convincing enough to fool a man like Sir Archibald, so
Betty can certainly be forgiven for being taken in. She says:

Bear in mind that the introduction came from someone I knew very
well and was well respected. Obviously he had been taken in as well.
The police interviewed me in regard of this man. I knew some of
the police because the social club where I was the secretary and
where I met Eddie was right across the street from a police station. It
was such a shocking experience and the effects continued on. I think
it was one of the things which recommended Eddie to me, because
I felt safe with him. He would have killed anyone who touched me.
I always said had I known what Heath's real name was then I could
have prevented the Wren being murdered. I never saw him again; he
got caught and was charged (and hanged) under his real name.

Coincidentally, McIndoe was treating the wife of another double
agent, one to whom Eddie was supposed to pass a transmitter. She
had been badly burned by one of the buzz bombs Eddie was valiantly
trying to divert.

As 1944 passed into 1945, the buzz bomb and V-1 menace receded.
So too did MI5's use for Eddie – although when it became obvious
that the Free Polish government in London was not going to get back
to Poland because the Soviets were installing their own communist
government, Eddie was 'engaged' to break into the safe in the Polish
Embassy in order to retrieve documents.

Meanwhile, the lure of London nightlife increasingly occupied his
attention. He later remarked, 'every plush club in town had a good cus-
tomer'. Soon enough, though, his thoughts turned to the young woman
he had so abruptly departed from in Jersey years before. He later wrote,
'Uppermost in my mind was the desire to find Betty, my girl whom I
had last seen when I dived through a hotel window before my arrest in
Jersey.' He engaged detectives to find her, but they drew a blank.

Lunching with his detectives at Berkeley Hotel, they reported their lack of success to Eddie. One of the detectives asked him, 'Is there anyone here who resembles her?'

Eddie pointed to a blonde with her back to him at the far end of the crowded dining room. 'That girl looks like her from the back,' Eddie said. Then, she turned slightly. 'Jesus! It is Betty!'

Eddie walked over and tapped her on the shoulder.

Betty takes up the story:

Peter used to phone me every night at six o'clock and tell me he was all right. One day he was shot down and Peter asked a fellow officer to call me so that I didn't panic. He rang me and asked where we should meet to tell me of the news. He had been shot out of the sky but was okay. We met in the Berkeley Hotel in Mayfair. Here I was, sitting once again in a long restaurant room with my back to the entrance, six years later.

It was a rainy day, and suddenly someone taps me on the shoulder and said, 'Hello'. I couldn't believe it – there was Eddie! I dropped my cup of coffee into my lap!

Just as her last moments with Eddie six years earlier had been punctuated with the sound of shattering crockery, so too were her first moments of reunion, as the cup rolled off her lap and shattered on the floor.

'Where did you spring from?' I asked. It was all I could think of to say. He was supposed to be dead! He said, 'over there', pointing at the back of the place. He was having lunch with a detective who he had engaged to find me, Doughy Baker. Eddie had looked around, got up, walked over to my table and tapped me on the shoulder … whereupon I nearly collapsed! He said 'I'm staying at Grosvenor House, Park Lane, call me.' I didn't think I would, but I did call him. And that's where it all began … again.

3

ROUND AND
ROUND SHE GOES

Betty ruefully comments that: 'Little did I know when I met Eddie that he would become my cross to bear for the rest of my life.' On Eddie's return, there was a song he used to sing to her in German, 'You are my heart's delight and where you are I long to be.' This was all very romantic, but by this time Peter Powell and Geoffrey de Havilland, Jr. were firmly in her life.

Betty recalls:

I did see Peter a few more times, but it was never the same. One time I went to a celebration with Peter and when I got back I was confronted by Eddie. He wasn't actually living with me then but he had a key to my apartment and I didn't expect him to be there! He was furious when I got home and he ripped all of my clothes off and locked me out of the apartment. This was a very upmarket building with several lords and ladies living there. There I was stark naked in the corridor, and I had to go and ask the rather stuffy porter to help me back in to my place. Eventually Eddie let me in, but not before the porter, Jeffs, had taken in the whole scene! It was hard to tell who was the more embarrassed, me or the porter.

De Havilland didn't escape Eddie's jealousy either. One day he came to tea at Betty's, and Eddie turned up unexpectedly. Because he was insanely jealous, she locked Geoffrey in the wardrobe. Eddie managed to find him. A punch-up ensued. But as was often the case, once Eddie's jealousy expended itself, he and Geoffrey became good friends. 'In later years if I ever retaliated for his infidelities by forming any sort of relationship, especially with males, he would become friends with them and that was the end. If they happened to be younger than me he would tell them my age, hoping to put them off.'

Just over a year later, de Havilland was to fly a prototype jet called the Swallow, which had been built to attempt to break the sound barrier for the first time. 'Eddie and I went up to Hyde Park to watch because he was going to fly over London,' Betty remembers. Just a short time before take-off, de Havilland had rung Betty. Her recollection of his last words is poignant, 'You know, Bets,' he said, 'I am getting too old for this game.' Minutes after passing over Hyde Park he was dead. As his aircraft accelerated, aerodynamic forces (unknown at the time) caused enormous vibrations in the aircraft, which then broke up over the Thames Estuary, killing de Havilland. Betty was the last person to speak to him. A friend who was staying with her and Eddie brought in the newspaper the next morning, and just handed it to her. The news about his crash was on the front page. It was the first she had heard about the accident.

Before Eddie married Betty she was also taken out from time to time by Jack Barclay, who owned the Rolls-Royce dealership on Berkeley Square. Jack Barclay used to send her enormous bunches of flowers from a florist right next to the Brompton Oratory. Eddie takes up the story:

I stood this for about four or five weeks and every day these bouquets were coming and what I used to do I would open the front window and fire them out into the middle of the street. We were right opposite the Brompton Church. Anyway I would wait until there was a wedding and I would fire these bouquets at the weddings. All the shopkeepers used to wait for the weddings and come out to watch. One day I caught his [Barclay's] car outside so I went behind it and I rammed it right up the back. I smashed the back right in. He jumped in his car and put his foot on the accelerator and every time he stopped I went right into the back of it. Then I rang him up and said 'Listen you dirty little bastard, if I ever catch you again near my girlfriend I will come round with a rusty nail and scratch every Rolls-Royce in your showroom.' The intercom was turned on in Jack Barclay's office, and everyone in the dealership heard it! And ever afterwards his friends would say 'How is rusty nail?'

Betty had another encounter with a serial killer at around that time:

I had a little dog, a little poodle called Peppy. I had been living in Queensgate [another expensive London area]. I booked into a hotel because I wanted to avoid Eddie. We'd been having battles and a friend of mine was over from America. I had had an operation on both my feet and couldn't walk properly, and my American friend wanted to help. It caused a lot of friction with Eddie so I wanted to stay away for the night. I stayed in the South Kensington Hotel, and during the night my little poodle piddled on my bed. The next day the hotel told me that I had to leave or get rid of the dog. I took Peppy for a walk to think about what to do, and as I walked out of the door I met this man who asked if he could give me a lift. I said 'No, thank you.' He had very startling, piercing eyes, and very dark hair. He asked me for a drink and I brushed him off. When I came back after my walk he was still there; he'd followed me around. I had to leave the hotel because of Peppy. I didn't know this at the time but this man was John George Haigh, and he had been charged with killing several women and putting them in an acid bath! He was very persistent but I am glad I didn't go and have a drink with him!

John George Haigh, commonly known as the 'Acid Bath Murderer', was an English serial killer during the 1940s. He claimed to have killed nine people, although he was convicted of the murders of six. He used acid as (he believed) a foolproof method of body disposal – dissolving their bodies in concentrated sulphuric acid. He then forged papers in order to sell their possessions and collect substantial sums of money. He was hanged on 10 August 1949. Betty had another run-in with a potential killer:

> One night when Eddie was there with me, a man who wanted to take me to America was outside with a gun and wanted to kill Eddie! He was going to shoot him and take me off to America. Exactly how he thought he was going to do that is not at all clear! Actually, after that night I never saw him again.

Even after Eddie's return, Betty and Eddie didn't move in together. In part, this was because he was always coming and going. The strains of the war hadn't helped Eddie's emotional balance. By her own admission, Betty was a little afraid of him. He could easily explode without warning: 'If anyone approached me in any way, Eddie would almost kill them,' Betty says. 'That was why I had to be so careful if I ever had any friendships that he never knew about, because he would have killed me and them too.' This was no idle fear. While before the war there is no evidence that Eddie had an inclination to violence (indeed, as a young man he won an award for saving a child's life), after the war, perhaps unsurprisingly given his experiences and his training, things had changed.

Betty recalls one particularly upsetting incident:

> We were once returning home from a party to celebrate VE Day with some friends, and we were in a car following another car when it stopped without warning and we ran into the back of it. Everyone got out of their cars and there were a lot of angry exchanges as to whose fault it was and finally the driver of the car in front turned to me and said, 'Why don't you just go home? I wouldn't mind going

home with you', whereupon all hell was let loose! Eddie didn't like the remark. A fight started and it ended up on the other side of the road in a shop next to Harrods. Eddie took one final swing and the poor fellow went through the window. Never another word was spoken on it.

Many such incidents would occur in their life, and as a result Betty tended to withdraw from social life. Inevitably this meant that Eddie strayed for companionship:

One time I found some underwear of Eddie's with another woman's lipstick marks on them, so it was my turn to be angry. I threw the underwear out of the window and they landed on a woman's head passing by! At that time we had a cat which actually belonged to the osteopath who treated Eddie. When I went down to retrieve the underwear, the woman said, 'There are very strange people living in this area these days.' Then she saw the cat I was carrying and went absolutely crazy about it. This lady had eleven cats herself and she was going off to America and taking some of the cats with her, going through so much trouble for it. We agreed to give her the cat, and then every day she used to call up and give us reports on the cat; how it had salmon for breakfast and the like. Eventually that cat ended up in America!

Of that time, Betty says:

Eddie was so restless after the war, I would never know what to expect. I couldn't deal with it but had to go along with it, although unlike his earlier life, he had me as a stabiliser. Our life together was exciting and adventurous, and oh so dangerous. But it was also disruptive because I always had some project on the go, and he would take me away from it. If Eddie went out drinking it could end up as three or four days of drinking and could end in blazing rows. One day he came home saying he had spent the night listening to music, mostly Mozart, with a young lady in Earls Court Square, my old friend Julie Cooper's best friend [Julie Cooper was the wife of the famous actor Terence

Cooper]. This became a habit. If he wasn't home, he would be spending the night in her flat listening to music. Supposedly.

When we were together and theoretically living a normal life, I got up in the morning but could never be sure where I would end my day! It could be Paris, Dublin, Rome, Brighton Beach, New York, or en route elsewhere. Otherwise it was a late breakfast and around lunchtime Eddie was on his way alone to meet a chum or have a drink in the local pub. I could be sitting around waiting for him for the rest of the day or even a couple of days or more – time had no meaning for Eddie.

But when we were together he was all attention, holding my hand and all that. He loved shopping for clothes for me or himself, and had a good dress sense; he loved me in flamboyant outfits, although I often wanted something simple and understated. He tended to want to show me off and we'd often row in our busy lives because it wasn't my style. Contradictory really because if any member of the opposite sex dare pay any attention to me he was ill tempered, it was not acceptable to him.

One male friend he was okay about was Colin Park.[1] I had become acquainted with him, and he was later the best man at our wedding. Once Eddie was going off to Paris to renew some acquaintances – no doubt female – and Colin said, 'Let's go to Ireland.' So we went off to Ireland. I wasn't romantically interested in him. He had booked the rooms in the hotel, but when we arrived I wasn't feeling well. Perhaps it was the journey. The doctor was called, and I was in bed. In came the doctor with Colin. The doctor asked what the matter was, and he had me strip right off. And there was Colin standing there who had never seen me undressed. The doctor said to him, 'Your wife couldn't be pregnant could she?' I thought, 'It would be the immaculate conception if I am!'

We actually stayed overnight and came back the next day, and in the meanwhile Eddie had returned from Paris. Eddie went to a place we knew called the Wellington in Knightsbridge. Colin had already gone there for some reason, and since he knew Eddie they both got very drunk together. Eddie had a French-made car at that time, and I don't think the drink-driving restrictions were as severe then, or Eddie would have never got into the car. The Wellington asked Eddie to take his friend out, as they were not going to serve him any more drink because he was too drunk. So, he took him out to the car, and found a card in his pocket to see that he was staying at the Mt. Royal Hotel. When they arrived at the Mt. Royal they refused to let them in because they were drunk. So, they gave him [Colin] his clothes and away they went.

They got back into the car and Colin said, 'Let me drive.' Eddie said 'no way', even though he was as drunk as Colin. He pleaded with Eddie and in the end Eddie let him drive. So, they were driving along Piccadilly, and they hit one of the big council bins alongside the road. The car went over several times and they wound up facing the opposite direction. When the police arrived they asked who was driving and Colin turned to Eddie. The policeman recognised Colin, and Colin said to him, 'I know you. You were my batman in Burma.' So, Colin was the golden boy, and Eddie was the villain. Eddie brought him home, where we had a big flat with a spare bedroom, and put him to bed. The following morning he said to me, 'By the way I brought a friend home last night, give him some breakfast, although he may not be feeling very well.'

So, I went in and to my surprise who should I see! Meanwhile Colin had told Eddie that he had been away for the weekend with a girlfriend who had given him the cold shoulder. Eddie said to him that he had been visiting old girlfriends in Paris, and they were chatting away. In the end it came out that it was me who he [Colin] had been away with, but because nothing had happened Eddie didn't get upset about it. In fact they were great friends and drinking buddies for a long time after.

Despite persistent proposals, Betty still had doubts about marrying Eddie:

Eddie had asked me to marry him every day for months, and I kept turning him down. I was getting tired of hearing it! He finally caught me at a weak moment and so I said yes. In the end I decided that life would be more interesting with him than without him. I guess I knew I ought not to tie myself to someone like Eddie. I did have reservations and I knew he wasn't really suitable. I realised almost at once I wasn't going to have anything like a 'normal' married life, but at the same time I found my life with him was exciting. So, I went ahead and tied the knot with him.

They were married on 9 October 1947, at Kensington Registry Office, which Betty describes as 'a cold, informal affair'.[2] She continues:

We made up for it with a great get-together afterwards with a few friends at my flat in Queensgate. I wore a lovely suit, as did Eddie. Our witnesses were Colin Park and another friend from an estate agent's near the Ritz. That evening after we married we went to The Little Club, before the party at my place in Knightsbridge for some drinks. It was all done in rather a hurry. Then we left for the country to spend a few days with a friend who owned a hotel, Frensham Ponds in Farnham, Surrey. It was intended to be a honeymoon of sorts, but I ended up helping out a lot because I knew the hotel business. Even so, it was therapeutic being there.

Prior to their marriage, in 1946, Eddie began writing his memoirs. Eddie's relationship with MI5, which was never the best, broke down towards the end of the war. He had contacts in Russia, mainly through Luba Dastier, which MI5 wanted him to exploit and obtain information, and which he refused to do. He also had a new handler at MI5 who took an instant dislike to Eddie, and was vigorously blackguarding him on the official records.

During the last few months of his work as an agent for MI5, he had casually informed his handlers that he was writing an autobiography. They went ballistic, and forcefully reminded Eddie of his obligations under the Official Secrets Act – that it would be impossible for him to disclose any of his wartime activities for a very long time. Not only that, but if he revealed any information about his criminal past, it might leave him open to prosecution. Eddie claimed he had never signed the Act, but complied nonetheless to the extent that he was going to write everything down while it was still fresh in his mind, but would not publish it. People working with sensitive information are commonly required to sign a statement to the effect that they agree to abide by the restrictions of the Act, popularly referred to as 'signing the Official Secrets Act'. But the Act is a law and not a contract, so individuals are bound by it whether or not they have signed it – signing it is more of a reminder than a commitment – thus Eddie was bound by it.

The idea of writing an autobiography started at some point in 1945 when Nye Bevan introduced Eddie to Sir Compton Mackenzie. He had been present at the VE night celebration, after which Eddie put the man through the window of Harrods. Aneurin 'Nye' Bevan was deputy leader of the British Labour Party from 1959 until his death in 1960. His most famous accomplishment came when, as Minister of Health in the post-war Attlee government, he spearheaded the establishment of the National Health Service. Compton Mackenzie is best known as a writer (his most famous book, *Whisky Galore!* (1947), was later made into a film). He was also a resolute poker of fun at the espionage establishment. A former intelligence officer himself, in his book *Water on the Brain* (1933), officers of MI5 and MI6 spent most of their time spying on each other. Mackenzie had built a house with a magnificent library on the Isle of Barra, an Atlantic island in the Outer Hebrides, where Eddie was invited to stay in order to write about his experiences, starting a manuscript in longhand. 'He went and stayed there for about six months, I think,' Betty recollects. He was also encouraged by another thorn in the pre-war intelligence establishment's side, Wilfred Macartney, who was once accused of being a Soviet agent, and became a regular visitor to the Chapman home. 'Oh, he was a crazy one,' Betty remembers. 'He would stand in our flat and be looking through the window towards the Brompton Oratory and shout, "I am God! I am God!" after he had been boozing.'

Eddie was warned by a friend that if he didn't destroy the manuscript that he had written with Compton Mackenzie, his life would be in danger. 'MI5 even raided our flat in Queen's Gate, looking for

Eddie's manuscript. What upset Eddie most was they took away his new suit and his new suitcase,' Betty says. MI5 eventually found the handwritten manuscript hidden in the flat and destroyed it. That, they hoped, was the end of the story. How wrong they were.

Some of Eddie's wartime experiences were serialised in a French newspaper in the spring of 1946. When the British newspaper *News of the World* tried to do the same, Eddie found himself in court in breach of the Official Secrets Act. British Intelligence brought a case against him, and John Ritchie, a well-known barrister at that time, represented Eddie. Later, Eddie got Frank Owen, the editor of the London *Evening Standard* newspaper, to rewrite it. As a consequence, it didn't have Eddie's name on it and didn't contain specific information. 'I don't remember how many thousands of copies went out before MI5 stopped the presses,' Betty recalls. 'The story was that it was the first time ever they had stopped the print-run at the beginning of a serialisation. Eventually the rewritten book was published, but due to the Official Secrets Act, the full story could not be told, and Eddie appeared to have been a traitor.'

When Eddie's book first came out, he went to lunch to celebrate with the actor Richard Burton at Les Ambassadeurs, in Hamilton Place, Park Lane. Betty remembers: 'I lunched at the same time with Elizabeth Taylor[3] and George Burns.[4] He seemed about 90 when I met him!' Eddie's book was then released and serialised in a French news-paper, *L'Etoile du Soir*. Betty remembers all too well those days:

> Whilst Eddie was staying with Mackenzie, his film *Whisky Galore!* was being made. I went to the Black Forest in Germany, investi-gating for Eddie's book. I found myself thinking about all of the German tanks going through the forest and it gave me such shivers. Conspiracy was rife, not by the press but by other people, so I was always careful who I spoke to and what I said.

With all of this going on, there was immense press intrusion. 'Eddie's notoriety brought endless people into our lives,' Betty recalls. 'The press were forever present. In many ways the media had contributed largely to our miseries.' She has a great deal to say about the press, even now:

Although we cannot bury our heads in the sand, the obsession with people's private lives has gone beyond acceptable, wrecking people's lives just for news. How can we fight for protection on one hand and then traumatise others with such media exposure? Trauma causes the mind to go into shock. Media manipulation distorts so much. Even when Eddie died, everyone clambered on the bandwagon to make money out of his exploits. It was a nightmare.

Betty has even stronger views about her own government:

Eddie was paid by the Germans but never the British; why give Eddie a bouquet with one hand and stick a knife in his back with another? He was treated so badly. I frequently became outraged at the character assassination of Eddie, which just seemed to go on and on. Perhaps I am wrong with my attitude, but I cannot forgive who-ever was responsible for the grief inflicted on Eddie throughout his life after the war until he died. So in the end the Germans were paying for his day-to-day existence. But the CIA and the FBI came to visit Eddie in London once the war was over to say how grateful they were to him, as his work also helped the Americans. I recently came across a note in Eddie's war records saying that he had been suggested for a decoration. Many people have since said that they will fight to get him the acknowledgement that he deserved but no one has kept their word.

People often ask me what life was like after the war with Eddie. Some mornings he would get up and say to me we're off to Paris, or Rome, or Tangier, or Dublin, or Brighton Beach; it could be the South of France, or any number of other places. Could be almost anywhere. And he would expect me to get up and get ready and get organised to go. No excuses, he just got up and went. I always had a project going, and it was difficult to just drop it. You never knew how long you were going to be away.

Their married life was far from blissful, although it had its brighter moments:

Eddie used to play away at times. I would get so lonely and down. I wouldn't say that I never interrogated Eddie on his return from one of his away trips. I would sit and tell him my news and then ask for his. At first no angry words; they would come later, sometimes a week or two. I then sifted through fact from fiction and so we went on. He only won his battles because I would consider what he had been through war-wise and had to come to terms with. But he surely took advantage of me and got away with nothing short of murder. After seven years of marriage, I became so lonely and seriously considered having a child. This would be the most far-reaching decision I would ever make. Eddie was quietly old-fashioned in many ways: he was courteous, but he expected me to perform all the duties of a wife for our whole time together, as well as propping him through all his business ventures. It was not at all unusual to get calls at all hours of the night to go to some sleazy nightclub to collect Eddie. One of these clubs was called the Maisonette. The woman who owned it would call me to say 'Come and get him, he's had enough.'

Betty continues: 'So in some ways when he left home to go away with one of his mistresses to carry on an affair, it was bliss time for me to rest and establish some order again.' In some of the more sensationalised accounts of Eddie's life, women – as much as danger – were said to be an addiction. Betty is typically frank. 'He had six mistresses in his life. And I used to say, when he was getting towards his end, "You know, you had all those mistresses. How I wish there was one here now who could help me with you!" This usually elicited a laugh.' Sometimes he would introduce her to people as 'my wife, Betty. She's lived through six mistresses, haven't you darling?' Annoying as this was to Betty, she would always smile and say 'yes'. When his MI5 files were declassified, Betty was disgusted when it was said 'that he slept with girls and gave them some disease'. The stuffy security services, and one man in particular, as revealed later, found every excuse to blacken Eddie's pre-war activities. 'He attracted women on the fringe of London society,' it was noted, 'indulged in violent affairs with them and then proceeded to blackmail them by producing compromising pictures taken by an accomplice. He confessed to an experiment in sodomy.' According to Betty, none of this is true. When this material was inserted into Eddie's files is uncertain, but it may well have been after the previously mentioned change of handlers.

Betty states:

Although Eddie treated me appallingly at times, all other times he treated me so well. He loved special occasions. Always when I had a birthday with Eddie he would take me out. One birthday Eddie bought me my broadtail flat fur coat and a pillbox hat with an ostrich feather. Mostly we went to Les Ambassadeurs in Park Lane for my birthdays.[5] One special birthday Eddie bought me some diamond clips that could be used as clothes clips or as earrings. They were very expensive and really nice. He was always very generous with his presents and would always think of something different. For him, birthdays went on for a long time. Our daughter is now a bit like that; it seems that she can never think of enough to give me. Eddie loved treating me in the Latin Quarter of Paris. There, Eddie and I used to go to a nude club. Eddie was forever trying to amuse or embarrass me and so he decided to take me there. I would sit by his side and the nude ladies would come and sit on Eddie's lap and fondle him in front of me! And I sat there trying to be grown up! Eddie once said that it was better to live one day as a tiger than a whole life as a lamb.

Another embarrassing moment also came in Paris:

We had a very special friend who lived in Paris, Cecile Robson. He had a small beautiful house in the city, surrounded by a brick wall. He had worked for British Intelligence hence he knew Eddie. I went to stay with him along with Eddie, and we were sitting in his library one day. I was looking at his paintings that surrounded the walls and there were a couple of what I considered to be very strange paintings that didn't make much sense to me. I asked Cecile what on earth they were. He said 'Betty, don't you know a Picasso when you see one?'

Apart from the fact that I grew very fond of Cecile, I loved going to his house to stay because he had a bathroom like one I had never ever seen before. It had every kind of perfume and bath oil that had ever been produced! The bedsheets were of the best pure silk, it was just like being in heaven! He also had real fur throws on the bed; it was a fabulous place to stay. It was a fantastic house, and garden as well. He knew all of the nightclubs in Paris and we'd always visit them together when we were there. Cecile's father, brother and sister-in-law lived in London, in St John's Wood.[6] One day Cecile and Eddie decided that they would send the father to the theatre with me, a George Black show I think it was. They dropped us off there and arranged a pick-up later. They wanted a bit of freedom as their dad was known for wandering off. One day, when their dad was staying down in the country, they couldn't find him as he had wandered away. They eventually found him in a freezer room trying to have an affair with a manicurist!

In the middle of the show, dad had his hand inside my blouse and was trying to undo it! I was doing my best to stop this and still watch the show. He didn't succeed, and he decided he had to go to the toilet. Off he went and he hadn't returned by the time the play ended. I searched everywhere for him, even with the help of the theatre staff. When Eddie and Cecile returned to pick us up, he still hadn't appeared. I am not sure where they found him; it may well have been in the actual toilet he'd gone to anyway! I'd never even thought to go into the men's toilet myself to check!

Betty remarks with classic English understatement: 'He was such a difficult man.'

Once Betty was asked what it was like for her when Eddie was away so long, either when he was with his mistresses or on some mysterious errand. Her reply was, 'I didn't let the grass grow!' The grass was not growing while Eddie was away in Ireland (see Chapter 4):

Whilst the shipping company was going on, I was having a minor flirtation with Keith Bedwell, who owned a place called Wigmore House on Wigmore Street in London, the headquarters of the Diners Club, which he started. I was meeting Kathleen Ryan,[7] an actress who was making *Odd Man Out* with James Mason.[8] We were going to Paris for the weekend together. Keith had his own aeroplane and said he would take us over. I think he thought it would be fun for all of us! Katy was looking forward to the idea, but the film was over-shot and running late so plans had to change for Katy.

So, Betty flew on to Paris where Bedwell had booked a suite in the Hotel George Cinq. Betty says, 'Now the Lord is my judge, he slept on the sofa, I slept in the bed.'

Back in England, Eddie's brother got wind of this: 'He told Eddie that I was playing games with him and was on my way to Paris with another man. I'd told Eddie I was going with Kathleen – as I was supposed to have been, until her filming over-ran.' With his jealousy rising, Eddie rang Kathleen's London hotel and spoke to her. Clearly she was not in Paris. Without waiting for further explanations, he then rang the Hotel Cinq to ask, 'Have you got a Mrs Chapman staying there?' When they said no, he made his way to Paris, convinced that Betty had registered under a false name.

When he eventually arrived, he contacted a friend from his days in France with the Germans, Armand Amalou, a newspaper reporter who was working as a mercenary. Betty recalls:

He said to Armand, 'You kill him and I'll kill her myself.' Fortunately, when he arrived I wasn't in the hotel, and Kathleen had arrived to join us earlier that morning. Eddie was boiling, but when he arrived, Keith had left on a business trip to buy timber. With Keith gone and Kathleen arrived, Eddie had nothing against me! I got left some money by Keith so that Kathleen and I could have a nice time in Paris. When Eddie joined us and calmed down, we all had a ball together. I have to say, Kathleen was in love with Eddie. And I was in love with her husband, who was the number one surgeon at the Limerick hospital!

Despite Eddie's explosive moments, underneath it all, Betty felt he had a good heart, and this was one of the things that caused her to stay with him. This was an opinion shared by many who knew Eddie later in life. And, whatever else might happen, 'life with him would never be dull'. One unexpected result of the *News of the World* furore was that they became celebrities. They mixed with the elite and became friends with Hollywood stars such as Stewart Granger, Richard Todd, Orson Welles and Burl Ives. The Rothschilds were a family that Eddie knew well.[9] 'One of the Rothschild women was even keen about Eddie' – Betty remarked with a chuckle. And, despite all the ups and downs in her life with Eddie, at the same time Betty was beginning to build up experience in business that would serve her very well in later life.

4

BEAUTY AND THE SEA

Betty battled to keep Eddie on the straight and narrow. After the war, Eddie still had some dubious friends; Betty had the benefit of a stable and happy home background and an innate morality. Villainy was always attractive to Eddie. Not for the money, but for the excitement. Betty was therefore constantly trying to channel his evident talent and ability into safer, legal projects.

Life with an unusual man like Eddie Chapman was bound to be full of challenges. A less self-contained and resilient woman than Betty would have given up at the first hurdle. But Betty was an unusual woman. Today she would have made it to the top in any calling she responded to. Yet the barriers to high achievement for a woman of her time were virtually insurmountable for most. Nevertheless, she persevered, albeit aided by the fame that came with marriage to Eddie, whose story was now emerging, bit by bit. Even so, she was on her own much of the time, and her achievements were hers alone. She looks back on the time:

I don't now know whether I would have chosen all the sudden changes in my life. If I had not been married to him, what would I have done? I don't know. I was driven by the fact that I was the one who had to keep on and keep things together. I began my married life looking for a way to bring stability to our lives. I suppose partly to portray a respectable life, although at the time I was motivated often by the money to live. There were several times when we were completely stonewalled up against it, and I always managed to find a way out, either persuading someone to help me start something, or persuade the banks to help me.

For instance, a simple thing: I saw a board advertising a property for sale one day, and it had the name of the company who owned the property. So I rang, and they asked me my name, and I said 'Miss Farmer' and he said 'Hello, darling', and he thought it was his wife, because his name was Palmer. He and I became very good friends – great friends. I don't think the relationship with his wife was very strong. And I got the property at a very reasonable price, and I was able to sell it and make a good profit. So when I managed to get the property in West Halkin Street, the agent was a friend – he was at our wedding, and it was through him that I got that house. I just happened to be fortunate.

Meanwhile Eddie returned to his life of socialising and so forth. When I found the West Halkin Street house, I was entitled to War Damage Benefit on it, and so I took it. I set about turning it into a paying proposition, and a home. It had four floors and I proceeded to turn two floors into offices. A society photographer was on one floor and shipping offices occupied the other. We lived on the top two floors. That was my first venture, my introduction to the property market.

I was also lucky to find in a nearby street a shop, which I turned into a hairdressing and beauty salon. Amongst our collection of friends was a hairdresser, who was also a dancer. At that time she became my partner in the business known as SIRI. We had an upmarket clientele, comprising lots of film, West End stage folk and so forth.

Eddie recalled of the time: 'I did exactly nothing. I just ate, drank and made merry.' This was to become a somewhat familiar pattern, although because of Eddie's injuries from his last parachute landing, he was never able to do heavy physical work. Before the war he had been very athletic. He loved sport and excelled at football, cricket, high jumping, etc.

Betty admits that she was never really a homemaker and was always busy with one enterprise or another. 'I loved property and I loved business,' she says. Despite her time on the Isle of Man training in the hotel business, in looking back to the early times after Eddie's return, Betty says:

I hadn't been trained in anything, except the school of life. But I think I was always destined to work hard; a soul needs to be heard. I loved walking; it was fantastic for my thinking process and was when I thought up a lot of my business ideas. God can contact us in many ways, and he helped me whilst I was walking, and thinking. Because I didn't have any particular skills, I became a sort of entrepreneur. As time went by I learnt from every venture I entered into, from inventing a pot of face cream, to building and renovating, to doing multi-million-pound deals.

SIRI was both a beauty salon and a hairdresser's. It was very rare in London to find a salon and beauty shop together, except Elizabeth Arden. It was a very successful shop located in a very exclusive area of Knightsbridge. One of our very regular customers was David Niven's wife, Jordis, and Tanya Mallet, and Sarah Churchill amongst other high-society names. Silvia Stuart was also a regular. She used to say: 'You know, Betty, my 'usband owns 'arleen's 'air tonic, but 'e don't 'ave an 'air on his 'ead!' She spoke very cockney and never pronounced 'h'! Harleen's hair tonic was very popular at the time. When I had the beauty parlour I was able to leave it with a manager. Her name was Adel Lawrence, and she had previously been a dancer. During the periods between dancing jobs, she had trained to become a beautician. It left me free to pursue other things.

At this time I was mostly involved in property. When the war was ending I saw a good future in the property market; it was all about finding properties that had been damaged by the bombs that could then be purchased with that as a benefit. War Damage Allowance made it good value. I had a marvellous bank that supported me to the hilt. I was lucky. After purchasing the properties I would reconstruct everything and then sell or let them. So I really was able to make money, really make money. The area I worked on was mostly around the exclusive areas of London: Belgravia, near Buckingham Palace, also in Knightsbridge and Victoria.

To further her beauty business, Betty took a course in cosmetics, leading her to invent the face cream mentioned above:

I invented it through an English doctor friend of mine. His name was Williams. We also invented a cream to make a coloured person's skin look lighter. I don't think we could sell that today! Eventually, I was made to take the face cream off the market. For some reason it was claimed that there was already another identical product on the market.

Betty's remark was: 'I'm damned if I know what it was!'
Eventually Eddie decided to re-enter the world of work. That is, work Eddie's style. He tells the story:

The Israelis were over here buying planes. At that time the war had stopped, but in order to keep jobs and the factories going they were still making planes. You could buy them for £3,000 or £4,000, without the armaments. They were offering £12,000. The moment these were built they scrapped them. There was an embargo placed. We were not allowed to fly these things out of the country, and you had to get special permissions to be able to use them. So I came up with an idea. I got an old drunken producer and said we were going to make a film on the Battle of Britain. We had a script written. We hired a camera crew, and said we wanted some shots of planes in action. Pearson flew one; George Dawson's pilot, Jimmy Swanston flew one; and there was one other. We got permission for them to be airborne and had the cameras there. We filmed the take-off, one after the other. Suddenly someone said, 'What time are they coming back?' I said 'They're not – they've gone to Israel!'

Soon after, Eddie decided to go back to sea. Having come from a seafaring family, when Eddie was young he was an apprentice in the shipping industry, at Thompson's Shipbuilders in Sunderland, north-east England. Based on this experience, he and Betty started a cargo business. Eddie and his brother Winston, a marine engineer, were in charge, carrying grain and commercial goods up and down the Bristol Channel.

They bought a boat called the *Sir James*, a coal steamer, from the Harris Shipyard in Appledore, on the north Devon coast.[1] This gave birth to the shipping and travel business called Courtline, of which Winston was the director. Betty and Eddie invested heavily in it, with money left over from Eddie's pay from the Germans, and from various different projects of Betty's.

In the early days the business consisted of the two brothers, a transient crew and one small steamer. Ever loyal, Betty followed them up and down the Devon coast as they shipped cargos back and forth. When work for small ships became thin, they moved to Newry in Northern Ireland and ran cargo from there to Glasgow. A transit office was built in Newry, where Betty worked for a while helping to arrange the manifests.

Although it is hard to recall, this was Northern Ireland before the Troubles,[2] but with all the problems brewing: a Catholic minority who found it hard to get work, idealist republicans who had not yet moved into the terrorist era, strident and prosperous Protestants who comprised the majority of the employers, and many ordinary working people who did not promote the religious divide. Eddie and Betty, never ones to take the Establishment line, found themselves friends with both the Protestant bosses who became their clients, and with the republicans. Before they could start the shipping line they had to drain a canal that hadn't been drained for ten years.

There was a lot of trouble with the IRA (Irish Republican Army) at that time, and the crew made it a point to be difficult, so it was a stressful time for Betty.

The crew was joined by Brendan Behan, an Irish poet, short story writer, novelist and playwright who wrote in both Irish and English. Behan was hiding out from the authorities: he was a republican and belonged to the Irish Republican Army,[3] and had been released from prison under a general amnesty for IRA prisoners in 1946. Aside from a short prison sentence he received in 1947 for his part in trying to break a fellow IRA member out of a Manchester jail, he effectively left the IRA. He wrote his first and much acclaimed play on board the *Sir James* – some of it on a toilet roll. In his memoirs, Behan refers to Eddie as 'the Fixer', suggesting that he was an agent for the Italians. 'I personally think that he was an agent for himself, but Scotland Yard gave him the benefit of the doubt and freedom from all his sins, past, present and future.'[4]

Eddie tells the story of hiring Brendan:

> He could write, and he was a very amusing companion. He could walk into a pub and take it over – start singing Irish rebel songs. He had a tremendous sense of humour. The friend who asked me to take him on was Kathleen Ryan's brother. He had never been to sea before, but I said don't worry about it. We only had four other people on board – myself, my brother, the skipper and a fireman. It was a small cargo boat – only carried about 200 tons. His [Behan's] parents lived in the slum district. We couldn't get a taxi, so we walked miles, right into the slum district. We went up a little hill to a row of broken-down cottages, and when we got there, it was about 2 o'clock in the morning. He banged on the door, and banged and banged. After about half an hour of banging and kicking and shouting, finally his father opened the window and shouted 'Who is it?' Brendan said 'It's Brendan, father. I'm going to sea with Eddie Chapman.' His father said, 'Good,' and put the window down.

Betty also remembers these times:

Brendan was one day painting the ship, from the bottom upwards and only then did he start to question how he was going to get down! Bill Beamish was the skipper and Eddie got on very well with him, they kept in touch and he later skippered Eddie's yacht, *Flamingo* (see Chapter 6). He was rather a drunk captain! On one trip, which turned out to be very rough seas, he came aboard with plenty of bottles of booze, but no food. Eddie made him catch fish and eat it raw when they were out to sea, as punishment, because he spent all his money allowances on alcohol.

It wasn't long after his stint as a seaman that Behan became famous as a playwright:

Eddie and I went to the first night of his play. He had an old dirty shirt, and a pint of Guinness. Many people had come to see him. People were buying him drinks, and he got drunk. Halfway through the play he suddenly shouted 'Stop! That's not the bloody way I wrote it.'

Eddie and Betty's business venture was not approved of by the authorities. They had opened up the harbour at Newry and were offering a cheaper and more convenient service than was previously offered to the farmers and traders who had to transport their goods via Belfast, which was further away. The vested interests exerted pressure on Stormont to bring in restrictions to hamper the business.[5] Eventually using subsidies, the rival company undercut and put Eddie and Betty out of business.

Betty says of the venture:

It was a hard slog. They did a lot of tough work to get the shipping thing going. Other shippers used to rip-off the merchants and, because of this, Eddie was able to cut their prices and carry the merchandise for much less, so that was a good start! Whilst in Ireland, I got ill and suffered a breakdown; I went to a nursing home called Saint John of God. Despite the severe rationing, the nuns used to smuggle beef across the border for me to eat to build up my strength. I then got transferred to Queen Mary's Hospital in London for five months. I really suffered from stress. It was a hard life with Eddie.

While Betty was recuperating, Eddie stayed in Ireland to run the shipping business. After its collapse he continued with the cargo business, but this time using an aeroplane. He had retained contacts with many former Battle of Britain pilots. Their expertise and undaunting courage, which had earned them accolades during the war, did not qualify them for anything during peacetime, however. So Eddie and some of 'the Few' ran cargo in and out of Tangier, which at that time was an international port.

Gradually Eddie's story was becoming known, and both Betty and Eddie became well-known personalities. Betty says:

Sometimes I look at celebrities and think how I know that scene only too well. At some point when Eddie wasn't around so much, I went to Paris for the weekend with a friend. Eddie told us to go to The Elysee and look up Johnny Zumbach who was the man that owned this club. We went in and sat down, made ourselves known, ready for some refreshments. I said to Johnny, 'That's not Aristotle Onassis[6] and Maria Callas[7] is it?' He took me over and introduced me and we had a good cosy drink and a chat. It was something that very few people have probably had the opportunity to do; they were among the most famous people of the time. To be certain they were more interested in each other than me, but even so I found them both to be very nice people. It was obvious that there was a very deep and loving relationship there. Maria sang with my friend, the famous opera singer Joan Carlyle, and Joan was later asked to unveil a bust of her in London.

We used to go quite a lot to Les Ambassadeurs in Park Lane when we were together in London again. I remember one time when we were there, Richard Burton[8] was having lunch with Eddie, and I with his then wife Sybil. We often lunched there to discuss the possibilities of making a film of Eddie's exploits. Sometimes we met with people such as Paul Douglas[9] and Audrey Hepburn,[10] and various producers. Audrey was so excited, as she was about to go off and do a film – she was all over the place! She was only about 20 at that time. We got invited everywhere because we too at that point were considered celebrities as well. To be quite honest we got sick of it sometimes. There came a time when we wished we could be free of the rich and the famous.

One of the rich and famous they had no desire to be away from was the actor Burl Ives,[11] who starred with Elizabeth Taylor in *Cat on a Hot Tin Roof* (1958):

He came to stay with us in Wilton Place in Belgravia. He was playing at the Café de Paris. He gave us a party there for our wedding anniversary. At the end of the party Eddie was seeing everyone off and Burl closed the door on Eddie, handed him some money and said 'Go and get yourself a room for the night.' Then he closed the door on him, leaving me with Burl inside. Of course he didn't stay out for the night, it was a great uproar, but it was a big laugh, we were all very good chums.

Of course, Eddie was fond of thinking up practical jokes and pranks himself, as well as his more dangerous escapades:

Whilst Eddie was around, he was always being the joker that he was, and once called up the undertaker and asked him to go to the home of Sir Peter Hodge, a well-known man at that time, and a good friend of ours, and measure up the body and prepare him for the burial! Imagine when the butler opened the door; he nearly fell flat on his face! Of course Peter Hodge was still alive. Eddie was always doing things like that, he was described as a loose cannon.

In the late 1940s Eddie went to Tangier where he bought a Beech aircraft with a group of ex-RAF pilots, including Graham Pearson, to transport lobsters to Spanish restaurants. This story began with Dennis Fox, a badly injured pilot who was in hospital with Eddie after the parachute landing where he hurt his back. Dennis introduced him to Graham Pearson who was also a pilot. They would use the plane for spotting. They would send the plane out to sweep the coast to see if everything was clear, checking for customs. They did some smuggling trips to Casablanca with gold, and some to France.

During this period between her marriage to Eddie and their departure for Ghana in 1951, among Betty's properties was a cafe in Battersea, just across the Thames in south London. She recalls: 'We had a manager who looked after the property. Eddie's many pals made it a meeting place, and always left the tab for Eddie. I was glad to pass on the restaurant, because I was having so many problems with staff, late hours, lots of travelling to and fro, and all else.'

She also owned a property in Brighton:

There was a betting shop next door to the furniture warehouse that we owned, and which we rented to a department store in Western Road in Brighton. They kept all of their furnishings stored there. It was a huge warehouse. There was a murder in the betting shop and in order to cover up evidence of the crime the betting shop was set alight. That in turn set fire to the warehouse, and since it was old furniture, it went up like a bomb. The warehouse was completely destroyed, and as it was underinsured I didn't know what to do. As a consequence, I decided to rebuild it using casual labour. As a consequence, I got a very intense education in building. This served me very well later in life.

All through this time Eddie remained friendly with many of his security handlers. 'They all kept in touch with him,' Betty says, 'though perhaps it was just to keep tabs on what he was up to.' Even at that time Betty was still not aware of the whole of Eddie's wartime activities. Eddie was full of stories, but he never divulged anything of consequence. A good line of chat got him through the war; keeping his mouth shut about important things kept him alive through it.

Indeed, much of the contact with MI5 wasn't just for old time's sake. 'They tried to use him when they could,' Betty adds. As previously mentioned, MI5 wanted Eddie to lift some important papers from the Polish Embassy. 'He cordoned off the whole of Belgrave Square where the embassy was located. He roped in some of his friends to collect road signs and place them strategically around the square, while he went about his task.'

Finally, at the start of the 1950s, Eddie and Betty (and Eddie in particular) came up against a task truly worthy of their talents: helping to build a new nation.

5

GHANA

Ghana clearly was a major interlude for both Betty and Eddie. In their many reminiscences about their life together, Ghana is the most often mentioned. In looking back over their history together, it is, perhaps, the time they were most together as a couple, working together for a common goal. It was a time of decolonisation, when the old imperial European powers, drained by the war, were unable or unwilling to exert the financial and military effort necessary to maintain their empires. Even the French, desperately attempting to hold on to their colony of French Indochina, were militarily defeated by the growing power of the native population – to found the country of Vietnam. Eddie would eventually fall foul of the French efforts to hold on to another of their colonies – Morocco. Eddie and Betty were caught in a tug of war between two powerful interests: the Ghanaians trying to extricate themselves from their colonial past and develop commercial relations with other countries, and the British struggling to hold on to a source of national income. Because the British were ready to reluctantly release their dominion over their colonies didn't necessarily mean they were ready to surrender their *influence* in those former colonies.

The modern country of Ghana is the former British colony of the Gold Coast. The Gold Coast was known for centuries as 'The White Man's Grave', because so many of the Europeans who emigrated there died of malaria and other tropical diseases. Originally a Dutch colony, the Dutch withdrew in 1874, after which Britain made the Gold Coast a protectorate. After the eventual conquest of the large Ashanti tribe at the turn of the twentieth century, the Gold Coast became a British colony. Even under colonial rule, the chiefs and people often resisted the policies of the British. After the Second World War, moves towards decolonisation intensified. In 1947, the newly formed United Gold Coast Convention (UGCC) called for 'self-government within the shortest possible time'. In 1948 the members of the UGCC were arrested, including the future prime minister and president, Kwame Nkrumah.

Nkrumah, born on the Gold Coast, went to the USA, where he received a BA from Lincoln University, Pennsylvania in 1939, and a Bachelor of Sacred Theology degree as well as a Master of Science from the same university in 1942; he received a Master of Arts in philosophy the following year. In the autumn of 1947 Nkrumah returned to the Gold Coast, where he was invited to serve as the general secretary to the UGCC.

Facing international protests and internal resistance, the British decided to leave the Gold Coast. The new Legislative Assembly met on 20 February 1951, with the now-released Nkrumah as Leader of Government Business. A year later, the constitution was amended to provide for a prime minister, and Nkrumah was elected to that post, with the country now adopting the name Ghana. It was during his travels related to the Gold Coast Convention that Nkrumah first met Eddie and Betty.

Eddie and Betty came to Ghana through an introduction by Lord Jersey's secretary. He rang Eddie one day and said that there was something he might be interested in from the Gold Coast. He said that there had been a revolution and a man called Kwame Nkrumah was in charge. He said that Nkrumah's representatives were talking about wanting houses, property and hospitals, and asked if Eddie could help. Nkrumah's representatives turned up at Betty and Eddie's flat, and said what they wanted. Then before they left, they asked if Eddie would speak to Nkrumah on the telephone, which he did. There was a great emphasis on getting the British out of the emerging nation of Ghana, Eddie was told. Nkrumah felt there had been massive corruption with building works that had already gone ahead by British firms. Despite having won a huge share of the popular vote while in prison for the cause, Nkrumah was hedged with the restrictions imposed by the former colonial masters, and was eager to break the economic stranglehold that Britain had over the country. Eddie Chapman was one of the means of doing this. Ghana was the first nation to emerge into self rule, and in successfully doing this the myth generated by Europeans – and believed by many Africans – that white dominance was part of some natural order, was blown apart.

For his part, Eddie knew of some concrete manufacturers and builders in Holland that were working with a revolutionary new process for forming concrete. He got himself introduced to the company, and went to Holland to visit them. Eddie outlined to them what Nkrumah had told him. 'When I saw their factories, they were huge,' he reported. 'They had rebuilt the whole of Rotterdam and Amsterdam.' It was all to be prefabricated, shipped out from Holland, and just bolted together when it reached Ghana. Once the components arrived in Ghana, they could build a house in about two days. The Dutch company, Schokbeton, was sold on the idea, and so was Nkrumah. Eddie was to go to Ghana to oversee, and was in for a good percentage of the huge contract.

The British were very opposed to the scheme because they did not want the Dutch in Ghana. Eddie remarked: 'There were only two British companies down there when we went there. There was Taylor Woodrow and Wimpy, and they shared all the building and contract work between them on a cost plus basis. Usually, cost plus quite a lot.' They did everything to keep the Dutch out. Eddie later reported: 'I had only been there a fortnight and they offered me £30,000 cash to leave the country.'' A point that Eddie and Betty failed to take into account was that Austerity Britain was still reeling from the Second World War, and was determined to hold on to commercial interests by any means, fair or foul. Historian Stephen E. Ambrose in *The World at War* remarked that Britain had nearly as much trouble recovering from victory as Germany did recovering from defeat.

But, Eddie had already got the bit between his teeth, and had finally found something worthy of his prodigious talents and abilities. As events would prove, Eddie and Betty made a small but nonetheless important contribution to the founding of a new nation. But at first, Betty wanted nothing to do with it: 'He [Eddie] came back one day and said "I'm going to Africa." I said, "Jolly good. I hope you don't expect *me* to go to Africa." "Oh, yes," he said, "Of course".' Eddie would later say of her: 'Betty covered herself in glory down there.'

Betty says of the time:

When Eddie was motivated, as he certainly was about Africa, nothing would deter him. He left and I joined him three months later. But even before I left I had had second thoughts. Before I went to Ghana I met a man who was a tea planter in Assam, India. He was home on leave and he was looking around for a wife to take back with him. We had a little bit of a romance, but I decided not to go with him and leave everything I knew, and instead to follow Eddie. I always had to be involved, although Eddie was often unaware that I was a woman, and how women fared in Ghana! At first I felt it was a mistake to have followed him, especially after I had made lots of money on my property and beauty ventures, but Eddie wanted me there for Christmas – romantic, perhaps; wise, maybe not. So, I left for Africa for the first time on Boxing Day 1951.

So started the saga of Ghana:

It took 23 hours to get to Lagos from London in a propeller plane. We had two stops: one in the desert at Dakar and then Lagos. As our plane touched down in late afternoon in Dakar for refuelling, the steps went down and in rushed several coloured fellows with sprays who proceeded to furiously fill the plane with foul-smelling fumes. I rushed out for the toilet and some water, close to collapsing, but when I got the only water that was available, it was warm. It was early morning and we were taken into a field to a wooden construction, which I suppose was meant to be the restaurant, for breakfast. Sitting there on the roof of the building was about a dozen vultures. I didn't want to get out of the bus which had taken us there, I was afraid they would attack me. When I did get into the hut, the sickly smell of paraffin (kerosene) was overwhelming, which did not fit well with breakfast! Paraffin was used to kill the bugs.

In fact, from the time I arrived it was nothing but bugs and beetles. If you had a drink you had to keep your hand over the top of it so that flying ants didn't land in it. The night I arrived in Lagos, Eddie and I and a couple of other men sat on a terrace near the airport watching other planes coming and going. I was wearing a fairly low-cut top, and when a big shiny beetle, a couple of inches long, flew at me it went straight down into my cleavage! Eddie was desperate to try and get this thing out. All the men were fumbling over me and I ended up being turned upside down and shaken. I had exactly the same experience when I went to Ashanti. At least my Ghana adventure *started* on a humorous note.

When we first arrived we lived in a hotel built by the government to service the traffic coming through the airports. It was called The Lisbon Hotel. It belonged to the airport, Pan American Airways used to come in there. We lived in huts behind the hotel's main building, it was gravel to get to the huts, and you needed Wellington boots if it had rained. The windows on the huts were just mesh. That was where I met the rat, Albert – he used to scare the stewardesses that stayed there. Albert was on the edge of my bed one time and Eddie threw his shoe at it and nearly scared me to death. It was a fearsome place. We lived in those huts for about six months until our company built and rented us a house.

One part of the hotel terrace was owned by Dan, and he sold lots of African things. Watching Dan selling all his things, always surrounded by people was fascinating. People just arriving in Africa were keen to buy something African and he was the first point of sale after arriving. This terrace was always full of gossip about who was doing what, to or with whom. The busiest nights there were the two nights a week when Pan American Airways landed, as everyone wanted to see who was arriving. Special receptions were sometimes given; Eddie and I had one as everyone knew that we had been asked to come to do some important work. The days were full but the nights more so: there were gatherings galore.

Betty describes what followed as a cultural shock, especially coming from a very wealthy part of London relatively untouched by the war. Seldom were white women found living in Ghana in the long term: it is not for nothing that Ghana was known as the white man's grave. Aside from the perils of disease, Betty soon discovered that it was a must to carry a cutlass in your car if you travelled, as she did, into isolated areas. Nevertheless, she found the country fascinating, even though at times frightening and even life-threatening:

After the initial shock, I committed myself to Ghana for two years and in doing so I had some incredible experiences indeed. Almost from the day we arrived we were up to our necks in Ghanaian politics. After getting to Ghana, we got together with Kwame Nkrumah almost immediately. Aside from our personal friendship with him, he was our contact for our building projects there. Yet over time in Africa, we lost everything we had, apart from a good friend in Kwame. I never ceased to be ashamed of the way that this country treated him. He was such a compassionate man that did so much for Ghana.

My most outstanding memories of Africa were the terrible poverty, mostly in the outlying villages; the hardships the women endured, while the men enjoyed lazing about. And the poorest of animal specimens; you could see them lying around everywhere, and you could see all their bones. There were bugs, bugs, bugs everywhere, open sewers, terrible smells – all embraced by red laterite dust.

All the way along the highways in Africa would be very tall proud cotton trees. If you stopped for anything on the roadside, people would come to sell you fish, you can imagine the smell in that heat! And these boxes of fish were covered in flies! They would also sell fruit, lots of plantain. But I'll never forget the smell of that foul fish. They were also selling pigs feet, sweet potatoes and homemade bread, but all covered in masses of flies! Water, though, was like gold dust; you had to sometimes get people to carry it for miles. Every village you passed as you travelled had guest houses that you could rent. I remember once going into a rest house and finding a snake under my pillow, so my rest period was over before it started! It was vital to carry a cutlass in your car as you travelled through isolated areas as we did, Africa was dangerous. Sacrifices were quite common in Ghana. Heads were at a premium. When a chief died, in theory they would be servants in the afterlife. Congestion on the roads was horrendous. Driving was a hazard, especially in the centre of cities where the congestion was appalling. The standard of driving was appalling as well. For a few pounds' bribe you could be passed fit to drive anything. If you passed an African on the road, he would spit at you and call you a pig, and being forced into the ditch was a game if you crossed an African driver. When this happened I just put my foot down and put my two fingers up.

Leprosy was widespread. Lepers were everywhere; people in the streets without arms and legs. There were even open sewers. Malaria was also a constant worry. In those days they didn't have the preventatives of today so it could have been life-threatening; here today and gone tomorrow. Because of the heat, if you died in the morning, you'd be buried by lunchtime. There was so much to remember to do to protect yourself, taking some pills, keeping out of the sunshine etc. It was hard to take all of this in after coming from London's Belgravia.[2] Ghana was completely uncivilised, no beauty parlours, nothing there at all. It was for me a great shock, from affluent Belgravia to Ghana was a massive leap, but I was forced to acclimatise and pretty rapidly too. Aside from the ever-present bugs, there was the heat; you could literally fry an egg on your car bonnet in the early morning! No shops, no dressmakers; there was just one big store. Everyone was wearing the same thing.

Eventually we got our house. It had a dining room and a sitting room on the ground floor, and on the next floor it had three bedrooms. The kitchen was outside, on a stove a bit like a barbecue. Eventually we qualified for an electric stove, meaning we had to be somebody of note, on a point system, so that was quite something. We had quite a nice garden. We lived there for about two years. We had house boys, like servants, and a garden boy, a cook and a night watchman to make sure no one tried to kill or rob us! It was common to sell stolen goods in Nima nearby; even the night watchman would do so. We trusted ours but still had to be careful. One night after meeting our managing director, who had come from Holland, we had to leave our car on the other side of our stream, swollen by heavy rains. Eddie had to drag me through the stream (between the road and our house) and I in evening clothes! When, the next morning, we went to get our car, all the wheels had been pinched! We had made some promotional films of the houses we were building, which had been left in storage cans in our car, but the films had been strewn all over the road.

Cooking facilities for most were primitive wood-burning stoves. We were fortunate to have an electric cooker, which was not always an advantage over the wood variety. Our Sudanese cook, Johnson, used to complain. In his words, 'the stove him kick so he not fit to use him'. Any electric items were unreliable because of installation. On one party evening with 250 guests our whole system blew up. We discovered a neighbour, a well-known government official, had had his supply connected to ours, overloading it.

Johnson was always at the palm wine. It was very potent. Cooks did not like 'the missus' going with them to the market place because they couldn't fiddle the money and buy palm wine. Johnson came home this day with the meat which I had already arranged for. He brought it inside in a tin while I was in the dining room. He banged it down on the table and looked murder at me and said 'I fit to kill you missus.' I said, 'Get out of here', and pushed him out and closed the door. He was in such a rage and crazy with the palm wine that no one in the house would do anything against him. I tried to get the houseboys to go out and phone Eddie, because I didn't know what he would do. No one could find Eddie, but eventually they did get out to get the government chief who lived next door. About two or three hours had passed and Johnson arrived with several of his buddies with long knives. Miraculously, at the same time Eddie returned home, and that was that. I couldn't charge Johnson because a white person, especially one in our particular position – for the African – couldn't really go against them. But we found another cook very quickly.

The new cook and the houseboys would come with me to the market. It had vegetables but they were expensive. You could get paw paws cheaper as they grew there, and also plantain. You had to buy your ice from an ice company every day to keep your fruit fresh, until eventually we got a fridge. When the chiefs in the north heard about this fantastic new innovation called a fridge, they went wild! So they all bought them and waited for the drinks to get cold. When this didn't happen, they said they didn't work, and they took them back. When they complained, they were told, 'Oh, you have no plugs.' Plugs were then purchased, and they returned to their village. They tried plugging them into the mud huts, just plugging the cable straight into the mud. Same routine: waited and waited. Until someone pointed out they had no electricity. The elders needed some pacifying.

Even our close friend Krobo Edusie wasn't immune.[3] He had a lovely modern house – smart toilet, facilities, bathrooms etc. Our first visit was after a long, hot, dirty journey, and oh, there was a lovely bath. I must say I was impressed by our bathroom until I discovered on turning on the tap that there was no water, and no plumbing.

Because the native Ghanaians had been kept as a servile people, they never had an opportunity to move beyond. Now that they were, at last, their own people, many of them were anxious to learn Western ways, especially among the emerging community leaders that Eddie and Betty were constantly mixing with. Eddie remembered the time that Betty had invited the wives of influential Ghanaians around to a traditional tea party. She had bought a new tea set. The wives all sat there, not knowing what to do. Betty put the cups and saucers out, and little cakes. She poured the tea and passed the teapot around, and they all copied her. Betty says of the time: 'They were very anxious to learn our ways, and after that we had tea parties all over the place.' To the pleasure and amusement of all, Betty also adopted some of their ways: 'They got me dressed up in Kente cloth, and made me the traditional African dress. When I went to tea, I had to wear this. It was long, and you could hardly move in it. It was like a long wrapover skirt.'

She continues:

When we were in the capital of Ghana, Accra, there was a store called Kingsway where you could buy everything except fruit and vegetables, which was sold by a different company called The Ice Company. Kingsway bought their merchandise in bulk. All the Africans that waited outside the store would then go in and buy stuff only to sell it again on the streets. Their main sale was cotton for clothing; the long, tunic-style clothes that were wrapped around. The market place was open and sold everything from goats and chickens to fresh salads. The trader's biggest problem was to protect their produce from insects: they wrapped everything in cabbage leaves.

From the market we would sometimes buy chickens and keep them in the garden, feeding them up until they were ready to eat. We also had turkeys ready to be killed and prepared for special occasions. I gave the houseboys whisky to give to the turkeys before they killed them so that it would relax them! One day when I looked out at the boys doing it, I saw them chopping off the turkey heads and drinking the whisky themselves! One day, the cook came in with a big fat chicken, trying to tell me it was from the market, but actually he had stolen it from next door!

The houseboys were both a source of amusement and annoyance at times. Once, Betty's houseboy, Peter, and the night watchman started fighting every two minutes when the Chapman's backs were turned.

It went on for about three or four days for no apparent reason, although it emerged that Peter had, unnoticed, stolen some money. Eddie mentioned it to Nkrumah, who said, 'Never mind, I will get the witch doctor down and he will find out what it's about.' When they told Peter and the watchman that they were going to get the juju man, the pair went absolutely mad. They were petrified. But the Chapmans told them: 'It's too late, we want to find out what's going on.' Betty says:

> So the juju man came up and he had some bones and God knows what with him and they were shaking like tapioca puddings. He gave them stones which they put in their hands and he then did his party piece with the bones and apparently he said to them 'The hand that took the money will be burnt' and my boy who was my personal servant suddenly let out a squawk and dropped it.

Betty has other stories about Peter:

> He used to come up every night with a drink. There were two doors to our room so if one door was locked on one side he would go round the other side. So this day I was standing in my room absolutely starkers and he walked in with a tray. I said 'Peter you knock before you come in.' So he held the tray in his hand, knocked on the inside of the door, looked me straight in the eye, and handed me the drink. On another evening we had people in for drinks. I asked Peter where Awini (another houseboy) was. He said: 'He gone piss ma'am.' I said: 'You must not say that Peter. You must say he has gone to the urinal.' So the next time I asked where Awini was he said: 'He go to the urinal to shit ma'am.'

She continues:

> The chiefs controlled much of the flow of money in the economy. But because they didn't trust anyone, the chiefs would get the money and then bury it. Then, they often couldn't find it again. There was about £20 million out of circulation, worth about twenty times that amount today.

When we first paid our rent I paid them in cash, but one month I paid by cheque, which had to go through a bank. A few weeks later I got a note from our landlords, saying 'Have you paid your rent?'

I said, 'Of course I have paid it.'

He said, 'Well, we haven't received any receipts for it.'

So we got hold of the chief and asked him if he had paid the money in. He said 'Yes, yes, hidden underground.' I said, 'You have got to pay them into the bank.'

He replied, '[I] don't trust the banks, missus.'

I loved the countryside and I never missed an opportunity to go to the government farm overseen by a charming (and good-looking young man), Tommy. It was about 40-50km from Accra, and approached by a very bumpy 3 or 4km track off the main highway. I found the only way to stay on it and to avoid toppling off the edge into the fields was to maintain a speed of 40mph. It did concentrate the mind because there were all sorts of assorted animals around. The farm was extensive and flat and reminded me of parts of Wiltshire. I just loved sitting with Tommy on the stool in the cool of the evening, swapping stories – gossiping I guess is more like it – as there was plenty to gossip about: who was cheating on whose husband or wife and who was sleeping around.

There was no shortage of local characters in Ghana either. Eddie recalls meeting one of them:

We went on the river there because the river leads right up to Ashanti. It has crocodiles and God knows what. At certain parts of it you have to be wound across the river on a chain-ferry and it takes about two hours to get across. When I arrived there was about an hour's wait and so I walked around. As you walk around the bank you disturb crocodiles and they dive into the water. I saw some Africans busy with an air pump. It was an old diver's kit and I saw some bubbles coming up. I thought 'What the hell is that?' because every now and again there would be a crocodile floating past and I thought 'He must be a brave bastard.'

So I waited and after about ten minutes he came up and the African jumped in and helped him out. They took his helmet off and underneath it was a white face. He looked at me and said, 'Hello, mate.' I said, 'What the hell are you doing?' He said, 'I'm taking samples for when they build the bridge here.' Anyway, we chatted and he said, 'I've got to go down once more.' He went down until he was completely submerged, and a crocodile came right over where he was. Suddenly he came up from the bottom and he punched the crocodile, and the bloody thing went about 6ft up in the air. He said, 'They are easy when you know how!'

Betty continues:

There was no shortage of social life for us. We sometimes had parties at our house as well as parties at other people's places; there was always something going on. Dinner parties of up to 20 and cocktail parties of up to 200 weren't unusual. Once Eddie and I gave a party on the same night as the governor, and we were over-attended as it was said that our food and drinks were superior. And, the governor had only cheap sherry! It ended up a well-known local joke.

Eddie used to go his own way much of the time in Ghana. But, says Betty:

If we went to anything official obviously I had to be there and if we had gatherings of course we would both be there. We had a string of coloured lights around the house and when we were at home they were always on and if we were not at home they were off. So everybody knew we were in and they would come around. We had a wide circle of friends.

Among these was the editor of *The Evening News*, and the owner of the cinema, who became close friends with Eddie. Eddie remembered him fondly: 'He was a great buddy of mine. I liked Fred because I could always talk to him, he was alone there. He would always listen to my stories. Every time I went to market and I would come back by, he would always have the coffee ready – sweet Turkish coffee in a china cup.'

Betty also has fond memories of him:

> When I went to the market, on the way back I would visit and he would bake me goodies and I'd sit in his garden and eat them. He also had a factory making tiles for the houses we were building, that's how we met him. He liked listening to Eddie's stories. One day his cinema burnt down, and the rumour went around that Eddie gave him the knowledge to build the bomb that blew up his cinema, but no one knew enough in those days about how to find out for sure. It was only really the Lebanese that had money there.

She continues:

> We used to go to another Lebanese man's beautiful house, where he had built an aviary with hundreds and hundreds of little birds. It was enchanting to sit there in the evenings and listen to the birds singing, I think it was one of our favourite places to go.
>
> The ex pats had their European Club, and it was very nice indeed. Sometimes they would have a special night in the European Club. The first time Eddie went, he met the manager who said to him: 'I suppose you will be joining our club?' Eddie asked him what went on there, and he said that they had dancing, various sports etc. – 'but we don't allow these black bastards in'. He brought Eddie some forms to fill in and Eddie told him, 'I'm sorry, I can't become a member.' When asked why not, Eddie said, 'I am here at the invitation of the Prime Minister and if I can't bring him to my club then it's not for me.'

Eddie went back to Nkrumah and told him the story. Nkrumah thanked him and then made Eddie and Betty honorary members of the African Club. Betty remembers that they didn't exactly fit anywhere into the old social structures:

> We were sort of a one-off because we went down to do something which no one else had ever done.

Sea View was the only nightclub in Accra, on the sea front. Anyone who was anyone visited the club. The walls were made of empty beer cases and the floor was tarpaulin. They had an old string band which was quite exciting and it motivated everyone to dance. Even the hot nights were fun. The toilets were made up of sheets of corrugated iron, full of holes, and you often would be standing or squatting to relieve yourself when you would spot an eye peering through a hole, over which you promptly put your hand! It really was a vast and different life that we went into – all because Eddie wanted the challenge of new things.

Lambadi Beach was a famous beach where we hired a beach hut which was exclusively for our use. We'd go whenever we wanted and we'd get the boys to go and get fruit from the trees; paw paws, pineapples and coconuts. It was a very nice way of spending time, swimming or sitting around on the beach and meeting new people. Once I was sitting on the beach and the water came in and took me back out to sea with it! Fortunately Eddie was around and was able to save me. They laid me down on the beach only to discover that I'd had too much sun and had sunstroke. I ended up in the Ridge Hospital. It was the only hospital with white sisters; the ordinary staff were still black. You could buy any amount of medicine for £5 from the nurses, provided that they weren't caught by the sisters! With £5 you could get almost anything in Ghana! The medicine could be very dangerous but also very welcome! I went to that hospital various times. I went once with dysentery; it's like a very, very bad tummy upset. It was terribly well known in Africa and was simply awful. We had to be very careful what we ate and drank. Everything was washed in Milton [a disinfectant] to disinfect fruit etc., but it tasted absolutely foul. In the hospital, the African angels came in handy with the painkillers!

One pain that even the African angels couldn't cure, was the way that Betty and Eddie were forced out of Ghana. 'Nkrumah told us never to both leave the country at once,' – as Britain would never allow us to return. He was right.

6

KWAME NKRUMAH, I PRESUME

Kwame Nkrumah made an enormous impression on Betty and Eddie, and they felt that the later problems he encountered were much more a result of people around him than of his own failings. This is more than just hyperbole. Eddie had circulated for years among ne'er-do-wells, and could spot a wrong 'un a mile away. The respect and admiration he expressed for Nkrumah was genuine: 'He was modelling his life on Ganchi. He was a very spiritual man.'

Nkrumah made a real effort to root out the corruption that was rife. If you approached a government official, he would say quite openly, 'How much you dash me?' i.e. how much bribe will you give me? Eddie gives an example:

For instance, I wanted water on the building site, and the minister said 'How much you dash me?' I said, 'I can't dash you, – it's your job.' But then you wouldn't get it. Then I went to Nkrumah and told him. Eventually he sacked the man who was in charge, but it was endemic and blatant, and it took a long time for them to get over this.

A strong friendship developed almost immediately between Nkrumah and the Chapmans:

> Our friend Nkrumah would always invite us everywhere and we became very well known in the country. He always tried to protect us in any way he could. We always had to be careful working in Ghana, we could only transmit for two hours a day,[1] and every time that we were on the radiophone, someone was listening in to try and scupper anything that we were doing. The British did not want the Dutch in Ghana, and our construction business was rooted in the Netherlands. It was not understood that we were trying to amalgamate the British firm Taylor Woodrow with the Royal Dutch firm we were working with.

Betty and Eddie always had to step carefully in Ghana as a result. They were, in effect, always being watched. A typical example occurred when Nkrumah asked them if they would go to Monrovia, Liberia, with him on a state visit. The Liberian president had sent his own yacht to Takoradi, the Ghanaian port, to pick up Nkrumah. Betty recalls: 'Eddie and I talked about it, and he said he would love to go, but he didn't think we dare go. We decided we would not go because it would cause such a scandal. So, he went off to Monrovia by himself.'

Because they were so close to Nkrumah, they were very careful to do nothing to embarrass him. One example of how close they were, was connected with that same trip. Betty tells the story:

> This is how well we were regarded by Nkrumah, how well he trusted us. When he was in Monrovia he sent me messages to say he wanted me to go to the French company who were representing the car people in Accra where he had ordered a new Cadillac, and could I go to them to collect the car. And, preferably, could either I or his chauffeur come with it to Takoradi to pick him up when the yacht returned. So, I went down to Accra and said that I had come to take delivery of the Prime Minister's car.
>
> 'Oh,' they said. 'Have you got the money?'
>
> I said 'Of course not, the Prime Minister will pay you.'

'Well,' they said, 'we won't release it without payment.'

I replied: 'I respectfully suggest that you do, because if you don't, I believe the consequences for you will be unpleasant.' So, after a lot of hemming and hawing they released it. I then went and bought his chauffeur a new uniform, but I didn't go to Takoradi because the press would be there and there would be a great fuss. They often used to say, 'I wonder what part Betty Chapman plays?'

In fact, Betty's input on Nkrumah's behalf was considerable: 'I took care of his household staff personnel, personally cleaned up and prepared and supervised the preparations when VIPs were visiting his house.' His house was described by Eddie as 'a glorified mud hut', yet that was of no consequence to him, or to Betty:

When we arrived in Ghana he was unmarried, and his own personal comfort seemed to be unimportant to him. He'd work so hard and get himself so run down, so I would send him milk and vitamins and be sure that his secretaries would be sure he had them every day. He was the head of the OAS (Organisation of African States, later the Organisation of African Unity), so some very highly placed people would visit. I'd always be present to help out, usually for government business, and I often stayed on as hostess for him.

He was very close to Eddie in particular. He would send for Eddie all hours of the day and night. It was nothing for him in the morning to say, 'Could you come now Eddie? It's urgent.' And Eddie would go up to his house, and if he had a problem he would discuss it with Eddie. Nearly every night he used to come over to our house as well. The night watchman would let him in. He would knock on our bedroom door. He had no idea of time. It would sometimes be 2 or 3 o'clock in the morning. He would open the door and say, 'Can I come in?' He was as bright as a daisy – he needed very little sleep. He would squat on the floor, whilst Eddie and I were under this huge mosquito net. He would say, 'Eddie, I have a problem.' Or, he would pick up the net and sit on the bed and talk. It meant that Eddie did more for that government than many of his [Nkrumah's] ministers.

At one point someone (Betty has her suspicions as to who) sent Nkrumah Eddie's police records. Nkrumah was unimpressed: 'I don't care what he has or hasn't done in the past. All I care about is what he does for my country in the present' was his response. What Eddie had done for Ghana was, in fact, quite a lot.

When Nkrumah became prime minister he was to do a speech, broadcast to the country:

> That morning he called Eddie and me asking us to go around to his house. When we got there Nkrumah was on his bed going through his speech. He read it out to us and then Eddie stayed with him all morning and they perfected it together. Once he had broadcast it, it was hailed as a great speech. No one knew that Eddie helped him with it, but we did.

She continues:

> Nkrumah called one morning with an unusual problem and said he was sending it to us: a mad Irishman had cycled all the way to Ghana from Ireland! So he arrived at our place, and we patched him up and packed him up with money and food and sent him off to South Africa with Nkrumah's gratitude. It was a stunt that only an Irishman could do.
>
> Nkrumah became one of my own closest and best friends. He once sent me 300 eggs from South Africa! I loved omelettes and he loved to come round to have some too. You never knew if the eggs were fresh if you got them in the market, so he was kind enough to send me so many! He loved nothing more than visiting us, and would always sit on the floor, often eating one of my omelettes!
>
> He also sometimes sent me huge baskets of every fruit known, flown in by air to me. Once when it was my birthday he asked Eddie if I would like a washing machine as a present, but Eddie said no. A washing machine was a lovely thought from a man weighed down with affairs of state. It was expensive and a real luxury in those days. He was very generous.

Another time, we were sleeping one night. All of a sudden there was the loudest jazz band bursting into tune outside. We woke up and I looked out of the window and the music stopped. We thought we were dreaming so we went back to bed and, as we were going to sleep, bang, up it struck again. Eddie stuck his head out – nothing. 'What the hell is going on?' he shouted. I woke up as it struck up again. There were trumpets playing, drums beating, the whole bloody lot. Then suddenly there was a burst of laughter. Nkrumah was having a rally where he had the Encruba Dance Band to play. He had given them £10 and said, 'Go and play outside Chapman's window.' In the end we got up and gave them all drinks, and some more money.

When he became prime minister, we were invited to the inauguration. We were privileged to watch the ceremony of the 'Pouring of the Libation', as it was known. We ended the day at a private party to celebrate his elevation, where only his ministers were present. We were the only white persons there. Nkrumah invited us to a rally of about 100,000 people in Accra one time, and when the Africans saw us sitting in the front row they all started to boo. Krobo Edusie, the government Chief Whip, as well as a great personal friend of Nkrumah, stood up and told everyone that we were good people and friends, and that we were not imperialists, and so at that everyone changed and started to cheer. 'Fire fire, fire, go fire the Band' was sung that day, as it was at all special occasions. It was a famous African celebratory song.

Krobo Edusie was also our neighbour, and we liked him a lot. He was a great orator. He was very humorous but sometimes a touch vicious. Once, on the terrace of the Lisbon Hotel, a beefy white chap, a Wimpy (construction company) foreman, said to Eddie, 'Why don't you put that bloody monkey of yours on a chain!?' He was talking about Krobo! Eddie had a few well-chosen words to say in reply and, informing him of who he was calling a monkey, suggested to him that he might be on his way out of the country before his feet could touch the ground. This incident indicated the fairly widespread feeling for the African. When the white community discovered we were installing indoor toilets in the houses we were building, there was a great deal of contempt for the idea. The general opinion was that the Africans would use them as wash basins or store coal or firewood in them. There was equally strong anti-white feeling, yet all clamoured to imitate, whether it be home, style, entertaining, education, etc.

Sir Emmanuel Quist was the speaker of the Ghana parliament known as the Secretariat. He was created OBE (Order of the British Empire) in 1942 and KBE (Knight of the British Empire) in 1952. The Speakers Conference Hall at the Ghanaian Parliament House has now been named after him. Lady Quist was an unusual lady to say the least, and once when I was in England she offered me one of their tickets for the coronation of Queen Elizabeth II at Westminster Abbey. I felt I couldn't accept even though I was in England for a wedding. Whilst in Ghana, I was frequently invited to their place for tea; I got on very well with them. He was white and she was coloured. Tea in their drawing room was the full works. She always called Sir Emmanuel 'Papa' and was seldom allowed to forget her past by Ghanaian society: she had been the delivery girl from the local bakery. One day while delivering bread to Sir Emmanuel she was found having sex with him on the kitchen table. The local saying was that 'he had his bread every day' – she was so pretty. There were many years difference in their ages, but it worked out just fine. Being the gentleman that he was, he protected her and sent her to England to do an extensive course which covered how to be a first-class hostess. He didn't want her to be looked down upon. So she kept a home fit for him and was good at entertaining.

The same friend that introduced Eddie to Nkrumah introduced him to the Dutch firm Schokbeton, with whom we did most of our business in Ghana. Eddie also met Joe Appiah, a member of the government with Nkrumah, and through him they all became buddies. While we were out there, Appiah met the daughter of Sir Stafford Cripps, the British Chancellor of the Exchequer, mainly remembered for his post-war austerity programme. They eventually got married. We were invited to the wedding but I was on my way back from Ghana and we got delayed so I missed the wedding in Kent.

Eddie also introduced Geoffrey Bing to Nkrumah, saying that he would make a good attorney – and he did indeed get the position as the Attorney General of Ghana.

While all of this was going on, Eddie still continued to be Eddie. One time he phoned up a hotel we were staying in and said that he was from the water board and that they should fill up any containers with as much water as possible as they were going to have to cut off the water supply. Eddie returned to the hotel to find every single member of staff filling up hundreds of pots and pans with water! Eddie rang our friend Mohamed Shaban at his brick and tile factory and said that he was calling from the telephone company, and that he'd heard there was smoke coming from his connection – and directed him to give it a tug. Eddie then said that there was still smoke emerging, and that Mohamed should tug harder. In the end Mohamed ripped the connection right out of the wall! One other time, Eddie told Mohamed he was from the revenue and that Mohamed had to pay a tax bill of £30,000, but that it must be paid in 50 pence pieces … by that afternoon! Mohamed actually went and got the hundred-weight plus of 50 pences and took them to the revenue. He was livid when he learnt of Eddie's trick! Eddie was always up to something.

Practical joking wasn't the only one of Eddie's traits that he brought to Ghana. Because I was unable to buy fashions in Accra I had a dressmaker named Maria who lived with a Lebanese. One day I went looking for Maria. Living nearby was a beautiful native woman named Angela. She lived in a mud hut, and men used to sell her to motorists. Many well-known locals were seen entering Angela's hut. That morning I didn't find Maria. I found Eddie, with Angela wrapped around him. In my usual style with those ladies, I gave her a dose of my feelings and left. As I got into my car she came towards me, followed by Eddie, and stuck her head in the window spitting out juju, much feared by Africans. Suddenly enough was enough. I promptly wound the window up, crushing her neck. She was screaming and Eddie was telling me to stop. Eddie warned me to back off. I let her go and made a very quick getaway in case Eddie decided to follow. Needless to say, feathers flew when he got home. You would have thought I was the one found wrapped around, the guilty one. Eddie had a great capacity for always turning the tables on me. His favourite expression was 'Always deny everything!'

Our business in Ghana was construction. We put in two and a half years' hard work building houses; the first permanent houses the Africans ever had, 238 houses in Ghana. There were eight building sites, and we were building all the time. When the white community heard that we were putting lavatories in, they were horrified. They said, 'It's too good for them. They won't know how to use them. They'll put chickens or coal or something in.' They designed and made the house components in Holland and then shipped them out to Ghana. The houses needed permanent foundations, but the buildings themselves were built in sections.

There was a lot of controversy about Schokbeton in the newspapers and Nkrumah said, 'What can we do about this?' Eddie said, 'The best thing we can do is for you to arrange for your ministers and members of parliament to come over to Holland. I can arrange for the company to pay for that.' So I rang the company up and explained what I wanted. Not only did they think it was a marvellous idea, it was the first official recognition of Nkrumah's government.

Eddie continues:

They sent a beautiful plane down, and took back a plane load of government ministers. When we arrived the bands were playing, and soldiers lined up. The Africans thought it was in their honour, but it wasn't. The Queen Juliana of Holland had just arrived as well.

I had asked them to wear their local costumes, which were beautiful. A lot of the material was made of real gold, made up in Ashanti. The Ashanti cloth was very expensive, as you can imagine.

The Queen was inspecting her troops when we landed, and all the reporters saw these Africans arrive, and they left the Queen to photograph us. She was very good-natured about it all, and we were taken down and entertained by her. Her daughters served us tea. It was quite splendid, really. And, it silenced the critics at home.

Betty continues the story:

Then Eddie went to the Middle East, Lebanon and Kuwait, leaving me in Ghana. He went to sell the same housing scheme over there. I had to go out to Holland to learn how the components were made whilst Eddie went to Lebanon. Eddie told me what to do and sent me to Utrecht, where the factory was. He said that I'd have to take care of everything whilst he was away. Nkrumah kept an eye on me and helped me. There were several newspapers coming in to see the things that were going on on our project, so I had to see them, and also to know the processes that had been carried out there. The British and the British government were very unpopular there so there was a lot of sabotage of the materials such as to the units and parts for the pre-fab houses. I had to supervise the building works with 2,000 native workers and only eight Dutch foremen, who spoke limited English and no native tongue. As an incentive bonus to workers, we instituted a daily pack of cigarettes and cigarette breaks. This caused a storm because the Africans all wanted to work for us and not other building companies. The British firms discovered we were giving the cigarette bonuses and they were losing their work-men, saying we were bribing them. So we had to stop it, meaning the workers went on strike to protest the loss of their bonus. When Eddie came back, the strike was still going on. Eddie joked about it and said I'd cocked it all up.

We also tried to do things on our own for local people. One village was right on top of a hill, and we had been walking for a few hours, about 11 miles, to reach it. At the bottom of the hill was a stream and the women would have to come down with their cans, fill them up, and walk back up. There was just one continuous stream of women walking up and down the hill. We met the chief and I said to the interpreter, 'Why don't you tell him that if he buys a little pump he could pump the water from down the hill up the hill and store the water up there.' All they would have to do would be to dig a big hole and cement it out. He explained this to the chief and he said, 'Oh, yes, yes. How can we do it?' I said he would have to dig a channel and explained it all to him. I said, 'If you do that I will send two men up and they will do the rest for you.' I rang back about a month later and they had done a beautiful job. We put a little petrol engine in, which pumped all the water up and stopped automatically when they wanted it to. They thought it was a miracle. The new cistern right on top of the hill was full of water. They were so delighted it was unbelievable. They weren't stupid. It's just that they were never shown how. You got satisfaction in doing these things.

One thing that the Chapmans were unable to do was provide all of their workers with bicycles:

In the promotional film for Schokbeton you saw the bicycles of the people going to work in the factory, and eating in the company canteens. When it was shown in the community centre for our African workers, everybody clapped and got very excited because they thought they were going to have bicycles and free food from the canteen. They couldn't understand that when the building programme started they weren't going to get all this. So I got left to sort a lot of this out when Eddie was in Lebanon.

She continues:

When we went on a break we stayed in rest houses. They were a kind of hut built for people that were travelling to have a break. Every now and then you'd stop off at one, and find a snake in your bed! The snakes were terrible, you had to wear snake boots wherever you walked. There were no roads as such, just tracks – there were so many potholes. When the rain came, the potholes would fill with water and in the season of laterite, the red dust storms, the holes would be full of red water and when it got on your windscreen, the wipers couldn't wipe it away. We drove whatever car that was available for us at that time. Land Rovers were quite popular. I made long trips to places like Kumasi Takaracks. I visited our building sites, which were long distances apart. It was often uncomfortable with the heat and you couldn't open your windows because the dust would choke you to say nothing of arriving looking like a Red Indian.[2] Being youngish and appearance conscious I would suffer to arrive looking good!

I passed through the villages with such mixed feelings, because I caused a bit of a stir with my white skin and long blonde hair. I was frequently referred to as the 'White Witch'. Often, if I was on foot anywhere, hordes of children would follow me screaming. I learned to carry coins and drop them, to the delight of the children who would scramble in the dust for them.

On one trip we went out gorilla photo-hunting in the mountains. We went out with the man who ran a newspaper called the *Evening News* for the government. It was very scary, way out in the wilderness. Eddie went up with the newsman to the top of a mountain to try and take photos. I got halfway up when a large bird flew right by me and scared me witless, so I ran back down the hill and stayed in the car. I was watching from down below to see if I could see anything and I did see two gorillas on the mountain top.

We built houses up and down the country so we visited various places like Takoradi, the port. Then we built the Tema Harbour in Accra, the capital. A lot still wasn't completed when we were forced to leave. A factory was under way as well when we left. The reason that they chose to use our method of building was because they had a lot of raw material in the country. The Dutch made the elements (concrete walls etc.) for Ghana to build a factory that could then make its own elements. We were involved in lots of projects while we were there, including a palace for King Premper of Ashanti. The Ashanti are a large and prominent tribe in Ghana, and were subdued by the British only after many battles. The former UN Secretary General, Kofi Annan, is half Ashanti. They did eventually build it, but only after we left. Eddie also represented the construction company Taylor Woodrow whilst in Ghana.

95

The Ashanti region of southern Ghana is a remnant of the Ashanti Empire, which was founded in the early seventeenth century. Its success depended on the trade in gold both with Europeans at the coast and with the Muslim north. In 1874 Britain annexed the whole region south of the Ashanti Empire as the Gold Coast Crown Colony. Eddie and Betty had good relations with the Ashantis, and were friendly with their king, Premper. Betty remembers him as:

> A fabulous character. The Ashantis at that time were a very war-like people. They are all about 5ft tall. If there is any trouble, it takes place up in Ashanti. But they are great people. The one nation that the British there were frightened of was the Ashantis. Ashanti was a fascinating bit of country and if you looked underneath it they were very nice people. One of our friends was a tribal secretary and his father had been a torturer to the precious King of the Ashantis. We met the king as well and we saw all his treasure.

Eddie has his own memories of the first contact with the Ashantis:

> This particular man was the chief spokesman for the parliament under Nkrumah. When I arrived he met me at the airport. He was dressed in Ashanti clothes. They have real gold thread, very, very colourful, and gold sandals. He looked up at me and I looked down. He put both hands on mine and said, 'You villain, me villain, we do business together!'

Eddie continues:

> There was an important Ashanti symbol of their religion, the Golden Stool and it is solid gold.[3] It takes about four men to lift it, and it is supposed to be inhabited by a white spirit – feminine. When I took Betty to the north, a lot of them had never seen a white person before, and they looked at her white hair, and they used to run screaming. They were petrified of her. People used to say to me, 'You can't take your wife up there – aren't you frightened for her?' I said, 'Frightened? You should see the natives – they're terrified of her!'

2 A picture of Betty taken during a photo shoot in the 1940s. (Chapman collection)

3 Eddie and Betty with baby daughter. (Chapman collection)

4 Shenley Lodge, a country house north of London. (Chapman collection)

5 Eddie on Lalandi Beach in Ghana. (Chapman collection)

6 Kilkea Castle in Ireland.
(Chapman collection)

7 Another view of Kilkea Castle. (Chapman collection)

8 A German newspaper clipping showing 'Eddie' being tied to a stake and awaiting the firing squad. (Chapman collection)

Eddie and Betty on their wedding day. (Chapman collection)

10 Eddie and Betty holidaying in the south of France. (Chapman collection)

11 Eddie and Betty on the beach with their daughter. (Chapman collection)

2 The famous post-war photo of Eddie in
SS uniform – which he never actually wore.
©Getty Images)

3 A still from the film *Triple Cross*, the
Eddie Chapman story, starring Christopher
Plummer as Eddie and Romy Schneider.
© Getty Images)

14 Burl Ives, a friend and guest of the Chapmans in London. (Wikimedia Commons)

15 Another friend of the Chapmans, the actor Richard Burton. (Wikimedia Commons)

The Adakassi was an Ashanti ritual that was performed every twenty-five years. It was to purify the Golden Stool, and its indwelling feminine spirit:

> They still had human sacrifice – that was the way that they purified it. It was still being practised. And they paraded all the entire house-hold treasures, like the golden keys, the silver keys. At night there were hundreds of drums drumming, and suddenly they would stop. Then they would start up again. Every time they stopped there was supposed to be a human sacrifice. They used to kidnap Nigerians, chop their heads off and pour the blood over the stool. Then there were two cases whilst we were there of young girls being kidnapped, and their hearts pulled out through the womb. Two of the people that were convicted had been educated in Oxford. The juju there was very strong. The people would adopt Christianity, and they loved it – the singing etc., but when it had finished they would change into their native clothes and go to the juju. People were terrified of the witch doctors, and would do anything not to upset them [as we saw in the previous chapter with Betty's houseboys]. They were so highly regarded by King Premper that he presented them with a replica of the Golden Stool – a singular honour never given to any white person.

Another person who they met in Ghana was Bob Flemming, who came to Ghana as the American Counsel General. He represented America in the Olympics for weightlifting. He sent for all his weights, and when they came, the porters tried to carry the box up the stairs at the hotel, but they couldn't budge it. Bob lifted it easily, and the word soon got around – thus his reputation was made. He corresponded with the Chapmans for many years after.

But their time in Ghana was not to last, as Betty recalls:

> While Eddie was still in Ghana, I came home to do something about a book that Eddie had written, trying to get it launched. On route home from Africa, we stopped in Dakar to refuel. While waiting,

as I wandered around an African sales pitch, a young African placed an ostrich egg in my hand, saying, 'You buy him ma'am, you get piccing' – that's a word in the African language that means baby. I bought it; my daughter was born soon after, after an earlier loss of a son. I also returned to England by the wish of Nkrumah to talk to the Taylor Woodrow construction company. The government in Africa didn't want us to transmit news (by telephone or radio) – so that no one could pinch the information – so instead they sent me.

Nkrumah had a big party for me to say goodbye just before I left for that trip to England, and he said then that Eddie and I must never both be out of Africa at the same time as Britain would never let us return; and look what happened! Asafo Ajah and her husband (who was the Minister of Agriculture) in Ghana, also gave me a farewell do at their home. I went down to the Congo, in Abidjan, and spent the night there, and very hairy it was too. The next day I took off for Paris. What I didn't know was that I was taking the inaugural African flight of The Comet – the world's first commercial jetliner. It had had a crash in Karachi just before, because birds had got into the engines. As a result, I was the only woman on board; all others had cancelled because they were afraid. When I got to Paris, I was greeted with a huge bouquet of flowers by someone from the airline. I was also given three days' stay in Paris for using the airline; it was great to be the only woman! I was anxious to get out of Ghana anyway. When I returned to London I stayed in Guy Gibson's old flat in Chelsea.[4]

The day before I was due to go back to Ghana, in 1953, I was staying with Eddie's sister, and two detectives from Scotland Yard came and said that my visa had been delayed and I couldn't go back until it had been cleared. So there started a real rumpus. Sir Richard Acland MP, a friend of Nkrumah, asked in parliament what had happened. They said they would have to look into it and let us know, and so delaying it as much as possible. Someone had said that we had given a bribe to Nkrumah and his party to get the contracts, and rumours started. Eddie was in a state of not knowing what to do, as we were apart with no contact, so he came to England to see me and to see what was going on. It was then that he discovered that a case had been brought against us. Eventually a 'white paper' completely exonerated us, but in the meantime, an English company got the contract. Just as planned, we suspected.

Eddie had a succinct comment on the whole affair: 'They were my friends. I didn't have to bribe them.'

There was also a plot to sully Eddie's name, which nearly succeeded. He was charged with robbing a naval man of £120 in the middle of the night. When arrested he had to empty his pockets. He had £2,000 in cash on him as he had been out gambling that afternoon. Betty recounts:

In fact that afternoon I had had a call from the woman who owned the gambling club to tell me that he had a considerable amount of money on him and was drunk and asked me to come and get him. Of course I did, I took him home and put him to bed. It was during this night that they said he had robbed this man of £120.

So then Eddie rang Len Burt, a former contact he had been working with from Special Branch. He asked him to come and see him, he came around and Eddie said, 'Your dear chief of police has framed me.' Burt replied: 'I had heard about you in the paper.' Eddie said to him, 'Len, I've worked with you before. Do you think I would do something like this? I can prove it right up to the bloody hilt that I was nowhere near there. He heard my side of the story.' Burt asked: 'Would you say that to the chief's face?' Eddie said he would. Burt said, 'Okay, I'll ring him now and get him round here now.' So he did.

Eddie continued: 'We were in this flat when he arrived and Burt said to me, "Repeat exactly what you told me", which I did.' The chief went absolutely white. Eddie said, 'This is absolute nonsense. I was never near the place.' He continued: 'Two of your detectives that were there when you were plotting and planning it are willing to come forward and say it was a frame up.' Eddie informed him: 'If I'm not out of court by Tuesday I will make it public and I will sue you.' He just said 'Oh!' and left. Len was head of Special Branch, and remarked:

'I know we've sunk to some pretty low depths at Scotland Yard.' Eddie went into court on Tuesday, and the Crown lawyer stood up and said: 'We wish to offer no further evidence in this case. A slight mistake has been made.'

A 'mistake' had been made, but the damage had been done – probably as intended all along. While Eddie and Betty were both tied up with legalities, an English firm got the contract they were trying for.

Betty recalls wistfully:

We didn't go back to Ghana, as there was no point. All we had had in the palm of our hands was gone. Nkrumah had to play along or else he could be seen as collaborating and there would have been trouble, but he came to England to personally tell us. He had been tricked into withdrawing my visa to save me from the embarrassment of being set up in a bribery scandal, which I never had any knowledge of.

   Back in England, following our Ghana saga, fame of a certain kind was awaiting us. One day I went to Claridge's in Mayfair, the famous hotel, and I had made front-page news because of it! It was splashed all over the front page of a newspaper lying in [the hotel] reception. It was also because I was Eddie's wife and my visa had just been withdrawn for Ghana. Britain loved to hate Eddie. Britain was always looking for something to charge Eddie with. It was all bad publicity – the British Establishment was always trying to discredit Eddie, especially to stop him going back to Ghana. Sir Lionel Thompson, a good friend of his, was often the one to bail Eddie out of such silly charges and put an end to the trouble.[5]

Betty and Eddie were back in Britain, cut off from their home and work, and despite Eddie's occasional luck at gambling, were virtually penniless.

7

A COLOURFUL BUNCH OF VILLAINS

Picking up the pieces after the disaster of Ghana, Eddie returned to Tangier and bought – with money provided by Betty – a yacht called *Flamingo*. At that time Betty owned a share of Terence Young's film *The Red Beret*,[1] which she sold to the film producer Cubby Broccoli in order to raise the money.[2]

She takes up the story:

Terence Young was very flamboyant and extravagant – he liked to show off. Although he made lots of money off the Bond movies, it seemed he was always short of money. One day he came to me and said 'Betty, I'm a little short of money. Would you like to buy my share in *The Red Beret*?' So I said yes, and I bought his share. Eddie had decided by this time that he wanted to get a boat. Eddie always had all kinds of wild schemes because his whole family was sea-going. This boat was the famous *Flamingo* that he went to Africa with, which caused press coverage more or less worldwide. Cubby Broccoli came to do the deal for Terence Young on *The Red Beret* and I immediately sent the money down to Tangier to help Eddie pay for the boat.

Eddie crewed the boat with Bill Beamish as his skipper again, and a crew of old criminal associates, as well as the boxer George Walker. Eddie recalled:

I had done a deal with the fellow who ran Soho to buy half a yacht,[3] an ex-admiralty boat. I had a look at it and liked it so bought a half share. I flew to Tangier with him and I met some friends of mine down there who said that they could give me one or two nice smuggling jobs. I said, 'Okay, I'll introduce you to the people running some of the smuggling, and there is a hell of a profit for cigarettes, whisky etc., and you can get plenty of money from this.'

Eddie said of his crew:

They were all villains, top villains, and not one of them had been to sea before. A lot of them had never been outside London before, but they took that boat 3,500 miles to Tangier. When the boat arrived in Tangier, they all got off, they looked around, and said, 'What the hell are we going to do here?' I said, 'Don't worry about it, I am going to take you to meet a friend of mine', and I took them to the best brothel in Tangier. The woman who ran it used to give me information from time to time. I introduced them all. They employed about thirty girls there. She had a menu printed, but as well as the food, was the price of all the girls.

They did genuine cargo work there, as well as the smuggling of guns, gold and cigarettes. Dealing in contraband in that area was so widespread it was almost respectable. Eddie tells the story: 'We ended up smuggling about 2–3,000 cases of cigarettes which we bought at about 4 pence per pack. The first trip we earned about 50,000 dollars. I took a newspaper reporter along and we sold the story to them.'

Most of this was unknown to Betty at the time, because Eddie said: 'I deliberately did not involve her in anything, for her own protection.' She says:

I didn't take part in any of that except that he wanted money. I had no working relationship with him. Some of those things that he talks about, I think they got up to some incredible high jinks. I sat there for three months not knowing any of what he was up to. The only news I got about him in that time was from the *Daily Express*, who were actually sitting there and watching me to see if I talked to anyone, waiting for Eddie to contact me. I used to sit on the beach in dark glasses and while away the time. I had no contact with him. I only knew what the *Express* told me or what I read in the papers.

The *Flamingo* had stirred a lot of interest in the British press and indeed Eddie took a *News of the World* reporter on board for some hair-raising activities:

Eddie only told me what he wanted me to know. I never knew for sure exactly what he was doing. It was for my protection. I was thinking that they were just taking gentle trips about the area in the yacht – until the newspapers got hold of it, and then it really became very, very scary, and I could not get away without them following. I was six months pregnant when he first took me to Tangier; I flew in to join him again, surrounded by press that wanted information on him.

Because of the crowd Eddie was mixing with, there was always an element of danger, even if Betty was unaware of it. It was brought home to her on one of their trips back to Tangier from London:

During this time I was once left behind in the hotel in Tangier because he feared that I might be kidnapped. He left a young man behind as a bodyguard, little more than a boy. I thought he couldn't have knocked over a weed. He hung around the hotel to see that I was all right, that nobody kidnapped me. This was due to Eddie's supposed attempt to kidnap the Sultan of Morocco. They got me up in the night and drove me to a Spanish airport to have me flown back to the UK.

Whilst in Tangier, we used to spend a lot of time at the yacht club, rather than the beach, which was opposite the Rif Hotel where we were staying. The yacht club had lovely gardens, as did our hotel. One day I wanted something from the pharmacy so I left Eddie at the yacht club and went on my way to find a pharmacy. I passed a man and asked him where I could find one, and so he told me to follow him just a few hundred yards. He went into some big double doors and through a courtyard and I followed him. I wasn't thinking properly. He told me he just had to pick something up. He went up some stairs into a lounge, and we'd hardly got in before he had me down on the couch and tried to get my clothes off. Fortunately I was wearing very tight trousers. I struggled and got my feet against the wall, trying to get free of him. I said out loud 'My God, my husband will be looking for me!' so that set the alarm bells ringing for him. He was caught off guard and I somehow managed to free myself and I flew out of the place and got away. It just so happened that Eddie had come looking for me. I told Eddie and, of course, he wanted to find the man and kill him, but by this time he had disappeared into thin air. It was difficult and not a very nice area. We'd go into a market place and you'd never know what you might find, you could buy anything and meet up with anyone.

We used to go down to Marrakech, where Churchill used to do his paintings. We did sightseeing there, it was beautiful. One day we got an invitation to go to the palace up in the mountains near Tangier, owned by the Woolworth heir Barbara Hutton.[4] Alas, she was taken ill so we never did go to see her for dinner. The mountains were very nice in that area. I don't know if it'd be anything that I would enjoy today, but I did enjoy it then. I remember being in the Rif Hotel when Eddie had gone off in his boat and I was accosted again by a young journalist. He offered me a shilling for every word that I would speak about Eddie and his boat. This kind of set the alarm bells ringing for me. I could always get news of Eddie through the press. Whatever was happening, he was always being quoted in the press.

She continues:

I was highly emotional when I discovered I was pregnant for the second time. I felt joy in one way, despair in another. Life would never be the same. Eddie was over the moon when I told him, but alternated throughout my pregnancy in moods of ups and downs. He drank much more than was good for him and I bore the brunt of the hangovers.

My first pregnancy was hard, and my first child died after a series of medical blunders. I had a gangrenous appendix and, when the child was born, it was strangled and died during birth because of the operation I'd had to have. These things must be why my second pregnancy was so emotional. And because Eddie didn't have any concept of what a woman's life was, he had no idea what I was going through, especially after doing so much hard work during the months of my pregnancy. Aneurin Bevan, the English Minister of Health, helped Eddie to find a good doctor to see me through the birth.

Meantime, we had rented a house in Montpelier Square, across the road from Harrods. The person who owned it was a well-known film director, Gordon Parry, and his wife Lucia. His daughter Natasha is married to Peter Brook, CBE, the award-winning director who did *The Lark*. Lucia was a lovely motherly lady of Russian origin and, from the moment she heard I was pregnant, she was kindness itself. Our apartment was on the top floor, good in a way for the exercise, but not for hauling up the shopping. I also had a lot of support from other friends. Rex Harrison[5] and Kay Kendall,[6] his partner at that time, were very interested in Eddie's exploits.

Another friend turned up during Betty's pregnancy: the former Luba Krasin, later Luba Dastier. One of Eddie's former girlfriends, Luba remained friends with both him and Betty for years after they were married. Before the war her father was Soviet Ambassador to France. Eddie met the beautiful Luba at a party, and within a short time they were living together. A question likely to remain forever unanswered is: how is it that Eddie was moving in the right circles in 1937 to meet an ambassador's daughter? By the end of the war Luba, still in touch with Eddie, was now divorced from her first husband, and had married Charles de Gaulle's right-hand man, General François d'Astier. As mentioned, Eddie's first ever publicity about his wartime activities came in 1946, when he wrote some articles for the French publication *L'Etoile du Soir*. As previously noted, MI5 went mad. What was less remarked on at the time was that the editor was Luba's son, Lalou. It was Eddie's connection with her that MI5 wanted to exploit.

The Chapmans and Luba frequently exchanged visits, and Betty says she was a charming girl and a very good friend to them both. In 1954, while waiting for Betty to give birth, and still dodging the press after the *Flamingo* affair, Eddie discovered that Luba was staying at the Ritz. In a typical Eddie Chapman gesture, he bought the entire contents of a flower stall, and had them sent to her. Although thoroughly delighted, when Eddie telephoned her later, she managed to whisper, 'Eddie, don't send any more flowers. D'Astier is truly jealous. It's very awkward.'

Betty returned to England slightly before Eddie, preparing to give birth. When Eddie returned, he arrived surreptitiously, and Betty met him on a road outside of London – all to dodge the ever-present press. The birth of their daughter was certainly a happy event, but was not untouched by drama. Because Betty had already lost one baby, they were taking all precautions. Betty had engaged a Swiss nurse and had organised the nursery. The press were still on Eddie and Betty's trail after the affair of the *Flamingo* and had camped outside the hospital. It was almost like watching a royal birth.

Totally unlike a royal birth, however, was the visit to the hospital of the Swiss nurse who felt it her duty to inform Betty that Eddie had moved a young lady into Montpelier Square and that his friend was also entertaining female company in the nursery! Betty discharged herself and took a taxi home. When she arrived, the nurse was running out of the flat screaming for help and for the police. Eddie had apparently found out that she had told Betty and had threatened to murder her. She evidently believed him, as she refused to come back to their employ and in fact took refuge in the Swiss Embassy. However, the marriage still survived: the nurse left; the baby came home; some degree of normality returned.

Betty says of the event:

Our daughter was born in The London Clinic in Devonshire Street in October. She was quite ill when she was born and was left in intensive care for about three weeks. When I finally left the clinic I had to be smuggled out of the back door because the press was around to get information. When she was well enough to come home, I wasn't able to take her home myself because of the hovering press; a nurse brought her to me. Just before my daughter arrived, I remarked to a friend that I felt I'd already lived a couple of lives. With Eddie, life was lived at fever pitch, the adrenalin working overtime. You were never sure what country would be next or what scheme was coming up. I guess after such a war he never ceased to look for excitement – and often of the dangerous kind.

Immediately after his daughter's birth, Eddie made a comment to the press that was widely reported, and widely criticised. His frustration with press harassment was only too obvious to anyone who knew him, but it looked bad in print. Eddie tells the story:

After our daughter was born, a reporter I knew said to me 'Eddie…' I cut him off there, since I had told him 'no interviews, and no photographs'. He said, 'Well, what is it?' I said, 'It's a little baby girl.' He said, 'What is she like?' I said, 'Well, like any newborn baby, she is like a pink skinned rabbit!' I mean, it was the first daft thing that came to mind. What did they do? They printed 'Eddie Chapman thinks his newborn daughter looks like a pink skinned rabbit'.

The press didn't stop there. Katy Ryan was a friend of Betty's, and she came to stay with Betty and was staying at Montpelier Square. Eddie had taken her to Les Ambassadeurs one night, and the press were there taking photographs, and they printed the headline 'Whilst Eddie Chapman's wife is in the hospital giving birth to their daughter, Eddie is seen at Les Ambassadeurs dancing with the glamorous actress Katherine Ryan'.

As the press saying goes: never mind the facts, just get the story.

The press were constantly after any story in which Eddie played a starring role. After Eddie had left Tangier to fly back to the UK, his yacht had been blown up, allegedly by French forces. Once, out to sea on the *Flamingo*, they encountered trouble with the engine so they entered a port and found a shipping repairs service. The manager said he would go and take a look at it, so he went on board putting a notice up in his office saying 'gone to lunch'. He got the boat going, and they kept on going until he got to Tangier, at which point he reported himself kidnapped! Eddie had also been asked (by someone with a political interest) to remove the Sultan of Morocco from the island of Madagascar,[7] but they could never get near to picking him up – so it seemed rather a coincidence that the yacht had been blown up. Eddie always blamed the French Security Services, but he was never certain if MI5 might have been behind it, although he didn't directly blame them. His exploits were international news. The destruction of the *Flamingo* even made it into the small-town American newspaper in Texas, the *Lubbock Evening Journal*:

> Eddie Chapman, retired safeblower, wartime spy and a gentleman who likes to keep the record straight, said Friday it wasn't true he planned to kidnap the deposed Sultan of Morocco. 'My mission to the Mediterranean was to pick up a few honest dollars as a smuggler. That's all', he said. 'Wild rumors preceded the arrival of the yacht,' he recalled with relish. 'We were there to rob banks ... we were going to burn the boats of the other smugglers. We had come to murder someone.'

While there was a large degree of buccaneering in Eddie's exploits in Morocco, there was also a touch of menace. Eddie tells the story:

> The local bank manager had been reported to have said that he was going to run those English bastards out of here, and I got fed up with hearing this so I said to the crew, 'Look, we will all go down to see him.' So we went down to this international bank. His name was on the door. We just opened the door and walked in. I said, 'Look, I am Eddie Chapman, this is Billy Hill and George Walker. This is my crew. What is all this rubbish about running us out of town?' I said, 'Any more nonsense from you, and we will get rid of you.' He said, 'No, I want to be friends.' I said, 'In that case we can do some business.' He called a meeting of the other smugglers and we agreed that we should have some of the business, otherwise we threatened to blow up all of the other boats.

Still, like many of Eddie's stories, this might be taken with a grain of salt. On a more down-to-earth footing, Betty continues:

> Soon after our daughter's birth, Robert Jacobs found a lot of property in London and Brighton, for me, Eddie and Terence Young. We had a house with a restaurant and living accommodation in Hammersmith. We let out the upper part and we owned the restaurant, getting people to run it for us. We had terraced houses in Fulham (south-west London), about twenty of them.

With a young child, life was a hard grind for Betty, with relatively little support from Eddie:

> He was really a semi-invalid. He was always on some sort of treatment for his back. He wasn't able to do any physical work at all. When we had all of the properties, I'd get up early in the morning and go round to some thirty-eight different flats, and they were spread out all over the place. I dealt with very heavy repayments for

mortgages, and heavy rents. There was always something I had to go down to Brighton for.

Eventually, the properties were split between Young and the Chapmans, with Young taking the London properties and the Chapmans taking the Brighton ones:

We took over the Brighton side of the property business. We lived in Brighton for about two years, the three of us, and our marvellous nurse who moved with us also, who was with us for about nine years, Marjorie Richards. She was a wonderful woman who told me to give up the 'filthy habit' of smoking. Our property business went on for some years and it ended up a disaster.

Jacobs had become a director of their company, and got them into a great deal of trouble:

He would sign for work to be done regardless of how it was going to be paid for. He signed thousands and thousands of pounds worth of orders for work to be done in London, Brighton and so on. We were listed as an investment company and when it came to pay the tax it was wrongly listed. Robert Jacobs had signed the forms for the work to be done, and since he was an official of the company, we were responsible for tax on the work which, in some cases was never done. The consequence was we lost a lot to the tax man, and it eventually put us under as far as those investments were concerned. Terence Young was the only one who made any money out of our properties, and he went on to make another of his Bond movies.

This seemed to become a pattern with Young. In the 1960s he would be the only one, according to Betty, to make money out of the film of Eddie's wartime activities, *Triple Cross*.

Eddie and Betty had gone into the antiques business as well in the late 1950s. 'I had to find something for Eddie to do,' Betty says. They opened a shop on the Kings Road in Fulham, Griffin Antiques, the stock of which came from a friend who was also an antiques dealer. Betty took out a loan to pay for the stock. 'I ran the antique shop for about a year,' Betty recounts. 'I quite enjoyed it because I got to know quite a bit about the business, the totters, and all that. Totters are people who pick up stuff. They buy it from the dustbin men, or they go round to auctions and pick up bits and pieces. Sometimes you get some really quite good small antiques from them from which you could earn quite a lot of money.'

Typically of Eddie, he had an affair with the dealer's girlfriend and moved in with her. To compensate the dealer for his 'loss', Eddie handed him the stock of the shop. 'So, there I was, no husband, no stock, a young child and a bank loan to repay,' Betty says with a smile. She can laugh about it today, but at the time it was serious.

This episode in Betty's life was difficult. She had to try to keep normality for the sake of her daughter, and she also had to generate an income since Eddie was in no position to maintain her. In fact, it was Betty who maintained Eddie and, amazingly, sent him money on a regular basis. Although she continued to be hurt by his infidelity and his cavalier treatment of her, she was becoming stronger. She was an extremely attractive woman and had no lack of admirers. She says herself that she has always been a romantic and, throughout her life, has fallen in love on a regular basis. However, she always fell short of the final step of commitment to someone else. This was partly her own sense of morality, partly – in the case of admirers who were married – a desire not to be the cause of another family's unhappiness, and partly a belief and fear that Eddie simply would not let her. However, looking back, she remarks with a degree of understatement that there were some pleasant interludes.

DOUBLE CROSS
ON *TRIPLE CROSS*

Betty always had a good head for business, but even she was not prepared for swimming with the sharks of the film industry, one of whom turned out to be one of Eddie's best friends. At the time that the negotiations for the film rights to Eddie's story were under way, Eddie and Betty were living separately. He was living in Rome with Mariella Novotny, and Betty was living in London and trying to pull the film deal together.

Betty takes up the story:

Despite continual interference from MI5, there was still hope of turning Eddie's story into a film. The company that owned the rights to Eddie's book was called 'Eddie and Betty Chapman literary properties Ltd.' Terence Young wanted to make the film of it. A company in France were also involved in the negotiations for the rights for the film. Even Alfred Hitchcock came from America wanting to buy the rights to the film, with Cary Grant to play Eddie. Richard Burton was also mentioned as a possibility. I met Hitchcock in London. For some reason he had to go to the American Embassy to have someone sworn to enable this meeting and such discussions to take place. In the end, he didn't buy the rights because Eddie had already met a man called Fred Feldkamp who also asked to make the film. Eddie had already done the deal with him, giving him an option to buy the rights for about £250. Feldkamp had the rights for about two years. He was trying to get people interested in putting up the money; he ended up selling the rights to masses of people. After making a killing selling the rights to *Triple Cross*, he formally declared himself bankrupt, I don't know how, but he did.

One time I had gone to New York to talk to Feldkamp, but the plane landed elsewhere due to bad weather, outside New York. I asked the reception if I could get a lift to Manhattan. I was alone. I heard the man say, 'Is there anyone here who would like to give a lift to Mrs Chapman to Manhattan?' A man offered to give me a lift and asked if I was anything to do with Eddie Chapman. I told him that he was my husband. I went with him and his girlfriend, we all went for dinner and that night he told me that his mother had been robbed of her entire savings by Feldkamp by trickery – buying some rights. We ended up at Trader Vic's, and we got absolutely legless and helped each other up the stairs back at the hotel.

This was about as much pleasure and reward as Betty ever got from the film. At the point where Feldkamp went bankrupt, Terence Young stepped in with a French banker to buy the rights. But the banker was also involved in some skulduggery over the US $6 million borrowed to make the film. He got into trouble with the bank, set fire to the bank vault containing all of the documents and contracts related to the film, and blew his brains out. 'So,' Betty says, 'Terence Young was left with so many people after his blood, he borrowed more money and made the film. No one that had the rights, nor us, ever got any money for it. Terence was the only person who made money. I could never understand that.' She continues:

Terence and Eddie were very close. I was invited to go to the chateau in France where *Triple Cross* was being filmed, a few hours from Paris. It was right up on a hill. I went with my daughter and Terence Young and on the way there we stopped in Paris and stayed at the George V. The following morning we were waiting to leave and there was this beautiful new Bentley outside with a chauffeur. I raised my eyebrows to Terence and he looked at me and said, 'Yes, it's mine, bought by *Triple Cross*'; in other words, they helped themselves to what they wanted from the budget. I was not to know at that point that Eddie and I would never see a penny from the film itself.

Because of continuing concerns over whether the British government might attempt legal action to prevent filming, *Triple Cross* was mainly filmed in France. The place chosen for location shooting, the Chateau Villascreaux, 70km south of Paris, had itself been used by various Nazi intelligence services during the war, and stood in for the Nantes *Stelle* where Eddie had trained for his sabotage operations.

Betty enthusiastically recalls: 'What was it like being on the set of *Triple Cross*? Fantastic! We were made a great fuss of. Terence Young wanted to use me for a shot in the film as Eddie's wife but Eddie said absolutely not! Yul Brynner,[1] who played Baron von Gröning, made a terrible fuss of our daughter.' Betty's daughter, coming from a famous family herself, was not about to be star-struck by Brynner, although she remembers him as a 'nice man'. What struck her in particular was that he watered his houseplants with bottled Evian mineral water, which she thought was 'rather odd'. Betty continues: 'We also liked Christopher Plummer's wife. She was a real sweetie. At some point whilst the film was being made Eddie received a call from the German ambassador of the time, telling him that it was his father that flew him into England.' Other members of the cast included Romy Schneider as the Countess,[2] Trevor Howard as the British Intelligence officer, and Claudine Auger as Paulette.[3] Betty remarks: 'Christopher Plummer was miscast as Eddie. He didn't even walk like Eddie. Eddie was very light on his feet and walked almost like a cat.'

Whilst the film was being made, Betty recalls that Eddie was sent to Greece:

> To keep him out of the way because there had already been so many stoppages. They didn't really want Eddie involved any more. He went with his friend Richard Johnson. They stopped at Rome on the way, stopping at a bathhouse en route that was run by nuns. A nun asked Eddie what he did and he said he was a writer. She said that she was also writing a book, about Our Father. Eddie said, 'Oh, what did your father do? Did he do something very special!?'

In his autobiography, Christopher Plummer said that Eddie was to have been a technical advisor on the film but the French authorities would not allow him in the country because he was still wanted over the alleged plot to kidnap the Sultan of Morocco during the *Flamingo* affair. Nevertheless, the film premiered in Paris and elsewhere, and Betty was there to see it:

> The premieres of *Triple Cross* started across the globe. I went to two, one in Paris with another fellow, along the Champs Elysees. The press went crazy at 'Madame Chapman!' when we arrived! Afterwards we had a party at a restaurant opposite. I took my daughter to Rome to another premiere, where Eddie was already, we went with a friend of ours who spoke Italian so he could translate. There we met Romy Schneider, who played one of the leads. When I went to the Rome premiere, there was Eddie sitting in the front row with Mariella and her husband. I couldn't get a seat because Eddie had put a stop on everything. In the end, I managed to get a seat on the front row next to him. Cameras all along the front row were frantically snapping. What a lovely picture for the family album: mistress, husband, mistress's husband, wife and daughter.

The London premiere of the film took place in the prosperous north London enclave of Golders Green at the very cinema – according to the film's publicity people – that the hero of the film had robbed thirty years before. 'Utter nonsense,' spits Betty. The studio publicity machine went into further overdrive: 'It is so fantastic, exciting and gripping it was feared if the story weren't handled properly, movie audiences would consider it just another far-out espionage tale…'.

Terence Young, arriving at the premiere, stated: 'It will make a hell of an exciting film.'

Actually, it didn't. For all the fulsome praise heaped on the film by the studio, the reviews were just the opposite: 'thoroughly dull and implausible' (*New Statesman*); 'unsatisfactory yarn' (*Sunday Mirror*); 'a rather shoddy, anachronistic, badly directed attempt to re-create one of the most thrilling of all war adventures' (*Observer*); 'double-crossed by the script' (*Sunday Express*).

Eddie had had enough of the whole business: 'I'm in the antiques business now and it can't hurt me,' is supposed to be his only recorded comment about the quality of the film. In private, he had only one word: 'crap'. 'The only thing hurting me is the fact that those stars have been paid so much money for making my story while I've received nothing,' he continued.

This wasn't strictly true. When it became obvious to Betty that there was going to be no return to her and Eddie from the film itself, she began a vigorous legal campaign to get the film stopped:

I engaged a lawyer in France and I suppose they also knew I wouldn't know much about the publishing of the film, so they just kept taking money and I kept going backwards and forwards. We had a few hearings and nothing came out of it until I ran out of money. My only recourse was then to go to the various places who were distributing it. We were always in the land of promises: it will be very successful and you can retire. Meantime, what they didn't know was that I had a roving husband who had taken off with someone, and he had a contract for personal appearances in America, for which he was being paid thirty to forty thousand pounds for doing masses of appearances on these different shows in America, like *Neil St John, Johnny Carson* and all sorts of shows. Eddie didn't *want* the film stopped. As long as he was getting money it didn't really bother him. He was the one that had run off and he was angry with me for trying to stop the film. He also had it splashed across the front page of the papers that I had stolen money from him. In the end, all my efforts really to try to stop the film were in vain. All I really ever got out of that was notoriety and aggravation. Everybody thought, 'My gosh, they must be rolling in it.' Later, the film was appearing all the time on television (and still is), but without money you can't stop these things. Lawyers are like sharks: when there is no more blood to be got there are no more words to be spoken.

And so, because of this, all the time I was on the other side trying to keep things going and trying to combat Eddie. It was more difficult at that time, also because Eddie and I were divided. He was happy that he had enough money to live the life he was living, and he did not have the same interest in fighting. Because I ran out of money I had to accept with gall, watching the film still being sold and knowing that we had not been paid.

I even got personally let down by Terence Young. I went to a number one hotel and when it was time to leave I said to the checkout, 'I will leave my account for Terence Young to pay.' So I left the bill. They tried to reach Terence in Rome but they couldn't reach him, so when I got to the airport I was arrested for non-payment of the hotel bill. Eddie had told Terence that he didn't have to pay the bill.

A year later, in 1967, Eddie got ill. He had worn himself out, Mariella had left him, and so I went to Rome and packed up all his belongings and brought him back to Shenley.

9

SHENLEY

I n 1959 Eddie had moved with the antique dealer's girlfriend to
Shenley Lodge, a large country house just north of London which,
at the time, was a guest house and for sale. He took it on a lease
and invited his friends. He also invited Betty, although he took care
to see that the girlfriend had temporarily moved out. Betty could
see the potential in the place, but it needed substantial improve-
ment. Eddie was too generous and attracted many hangers on. The
local constabulary started to take interest in some of the guests who
descended on the club – a great many of whom were Eddie's underworld cronies. Eventually the money ran out and Eddie left for the
Continent with yet another mistress. Betty took over what remained
of the lease and started to make plans. Against considerable odds, she
managed to borrow the money to start refurbishment. Naturally she
had to do all the financial dealings. She suffered several setbacks, one
of which was to be arrested shortly after Eddie's departure and taken
to the local magistrate's court for non-payment of rates (property
tax), which Eddie had neglected to pay. Eventually, to rid herself of

the undesirables who had been attracted to the place, she gave up the drinks licence.

Betty remembers the time:

We got a licence to sell drinks, which was a disaster really because all of Eddie's friends came in and drank the profits. They took the licence away from Eddie in 1960, so I had to take over Shenley in order to get the licence back. We turned it into a country club, a place where people could come and stay and eat and drink all night. If you came in just as a member you could only drink until about 11 p.m.

Eventually, after a lot of research and hard work, and with Eddie coming and going, we turned it into a health farm. My journey of discovery into the health farm world took me to France, Germany, Switzerland and America. I was acquainted with the beauty side of the business from my early years in Belgravia. But such treatments as hydrotherapy and the latest methods of exercise and therapies I was not familiar with, and slimming had become big business. We used to have special diets, physical training, plunge pools, saunas, massage and many kinds of treatment. It took a number of us a good couple of years to get it all set up.

Lilian Verner-Bonds described the completed Shenley Lodge as 'an enchanting place, not like a traditional health farm. Eddie had a habit of making each and every one feel special. He and Betty were the perfect double-act.'[1]

Because she was new to slimming, Betty asked for and got some good advice. She was told that the best kind of advert is to get a very big woman who looks shabby, photograph her, put her through her paces to lose weight, and then go and buy a very nice dress and have the photograph done again. She was told that if she did that, she had to certify that it was true. She had to get a lawyer in, and do what she said she was going to do. Today, such a procedure would be obvious. Then, it was revolutionary.

Betty remembers:

We had some pretty well-known characters there. We had a good connection with nearby Elstree Film Studios, and the people filming there would come and stay with us.[2] We made quite a big gymnasium open to the public and Roger Moore (better known later for his portrayal of James Bond) used to come and work out there during the filming of *The Saint*. Diana Rigg and Patrick Macnee stayed during the filming of *The Avengers*, Patrick Wymark during *The Power Game*.[3] Robert Mitchum, Trevor Howard and Elspeth March are amongst other names that stayed there. Whilst we were at Shenley it was used as a location for the film *A Clockwork Orange* and the TV show *Inspector Morse*. There were also a lot of sportsmen staying with us at Shenley. The boxer John Conteh did most of his training there.[4]

When Arab families came to Shenley there were two separate areas, one for men and one for women and they were completely segregated. This makes one of Betty's stories more remarkable:

The young Prince Ali Althani of Qatar was a regular visitor to Shenley. On one of his visits, the daughters of a well-known cartoonist with *El Ahram* newspaper in Egypt, Amina, who was 16, and Magda who was 17, were staying with us. We heard loud giggles coming from his room, and we realised what was going on. Ali had the girls in his room showing them a pornographic film. What was so amazing was that Ali told us he was showing the girls a film of his country!

Once Ali left for a trip with Olga's son Alex in his car. Olga was Eddie's younger sister. She was a great character and a real survivor. She worked at the health farm on the reception desk for years. She was a real optimist and always managed to make the best of any situation. While speeding along a main highway, Ali and Alex trailed a clothing store mannequin's limbs out of the car window. I have no idea where they got it. A police car spotted it, and thought it was a real body. They were both arrested after police found a gun on the window ledge. I was summoned to the local police station, where I pleaded for the young sheik. I had to make a lengthy statement some days later, explaining away his high spirits. I managed to finally convince the police of his innocence of any law-breaking intentions. He was indeed a handful, but I truly missed him when he died at the age of around 20, having spent many years with us. In fact, his mother used to say, 'Go home to your English mother,' when he was really out of hand in Qatar. When he had visitors at Shenley he always introduced me, with a twinkle in his eye, as his mother – often to raised eyebrows. We were very close.

Lila, one of our favourites, was another young Arab client at Shenley who was a long-stay patient sent by her parents to lose weight. Her father had left gift boxes of chocolates for the staff. One day we found her on the flat part of the roof, flinging the empty boxes over the side, having (of course) consumed all the chocolate.

The royal families of Iran, Jordan and Qatar enjoyed happy times there and kept in contact with me long after. We were noted for our care of young Middle Eastern people, who mainly came to England for serious operations. One family whose son was in Britain for major surgery came prepared to stay for several months – after a week they left happy in the knowledge he would now be safe and happy with us. We visited him regularly in his London hospital, comforting him when he was sad. He made a spectacular recovery. One Libyan general's wife stayed with us for a year after an appendectomy.

The heiress Henrietta Guinness spent a lot of time with Betty and Eddie at Shenley.[5] Betty was very sympathetic to Henrietta:

I think she was terribly mixed up and desperate for affection. She spent the last Christmas with us before she died. She said that it was the happiest Christmas that she had ever spent because we put things on the tree for her. I remember giving her some knickers and tights and she took everything off and put them on, and thought that it was absolutely fabulous that she was treated like a normal person. She came back and forwards to Shenley like a homing pigeon. She left to visit the man she had a child with in the Middle East somewhere. She became pregnant by this man, whose mother was a chamber maid in a hotel. One day she was very depressed and jumped 250ft from a bridge and killed herself. That was a shattering blow to me – when you know someone for a long time and something like that happens, it's just devastating.

Captain Dusty Rhoads, from the American Air Force came to stay with us whilst his plane was being serviced at the de Havilland aviation facility in Hatfield – the place that Eddie was supposed to have blown up during the war! He had such a wonderful time at Shenley that he said he wanted to be buried there! We had a lovely lunch, which I can still picture today. We were all giggling and really enjoying ourselves. Then he had to go to pick up the plane again, and collect an Arab king's wife who had been holidaying in the Pyrenees. After he picked them up with all their jewels and clothing, the plane crashed and they all lost their lives. That was one of the hardest days for me.

That wasn't the only hard day for Betty, not by a million miles. By the time the refurbishment was completed, Eddie had met Mariella Novotny. Betty recounts: 'She used to sneak in to stay with him whilst I was in London. I knew about it since the staff kept me informed; Eddie's sister was our receptionist. Eddie always denied the affair. But he went to Rome on a short trip with her, and ended up staying a while.' Years, in fact.

Mariella was up to her neck in the national scandal of the day, the Profumo Affair.[6] A Marilyn Monroe lookalike, she became a strip-tease dancer, supposedly to support her widowed mother. Novotny also worked as a prostitute in London. Another major participant in the Profumo Affair, Christine Keeler, reported that, 'She was a siren, a sexual athlete of Olympian proportions – she could do it all. I know. I saw her in action.'[7] In 1960 she married Horace Dibben, a wealthy antiques dealer and nightclub owner thirty-six years her senior. Her engagement ring was an antique 200-year-old diamond and sapphire confection. Novotny travelled to the United States in 1961, and was arrested by the FBI and charged with soliciting for prostitution.

She was also of interest to the FBI in no small part because she came under investigation for having claimed to have slept with President Kennedy. Within a few weeks she had slipped out of the country using a false name and returned to Britain, where she once again took up running sex parties in London, along with her husband.

There is no suggestion that Eddie ever attended one of these parties. It is likely that he met Mariella through his osteopath, Stephen Ward, another major figure in the Profumo Affair. Ward had been Eddie's osteopath for some time, giving him treatment for the back injuries he had suffered during his last parachute drop into England on behalf of the Germans. Eddie had been shoved out of the plane and became entangled in his parachute, and landed very badly on his back on a concrete path. He and Stephen Ward used to go drinking together: they often went to a famous pub called The Star. Ward travelled in society circles, and was a key player in introducing various girls such as Novotny and Keeler to high-up political figures like Profumo. Betty remembers Ward well: 'Stephen had a cat and he gave us this damned cat as a present, and it used to poop in the bath. I remember Eddie and I had a terrible row about it.' This is the cat that Betty gave away after tossing Eddie's clothes out of the window (as recounted in Chapter 3). In the end, Stephen Ward was prosecuted for living on the immoral earnings of prostitution; he committed suicide in August 1963. Betty says: 'It was a terrible shock when Stephen committed suicide – I'm sure he was driven to it.'

During the time in the 1960s when Eddie and Betty were living apart, she was kept very busy with Shenley, so her life was very full. Eddie spent much of that time in Rome with Mariella, and also living in a house in Hyde Park Square with both Mariella and her husband. Betty was still financing a certain part of his lifestyle, although he did have some funds from selling the rights to the film *Triple Cross*, which was what he was living off in Rome, as well as his fees for television appearances. When asked if she wondered whether or not Eddie would ever come back, Betty replied:

I did miss him but he was that kind of person. I knew that when we married. We had a good physical relationship but many women were also attracted to him. I always knew he would come back and he always did [...] Her [Mariella's] mother even used to ring me up, wondering what to do. She said: 'She's got a whole trunk of whips in the basement. What do I do?' I said, 'Get rid of it.' Her mother Connie was a truly sweet lady, who felt sorry for me being deserted for her daughter. She kept me up to date with news of her and my husband's whereabouts. She walked miles to telephone boxes to speak to me secretly.

To Betty's disgust, Eddie brought Mariella to the grand reopening of Shenley Lodge as a health farm. She even sat on the front desk at Shenley posing for photographs. In fact, he had *two* mistresses there. Betty recounts:

I had a personal assistant who was engaged to help me with the health farm. His job that night was to keep the two mistresses apart. I knew them, and who they were. One of them even gave me two dozen roses. One day she rang up and asked Eddie if she could speak to me. She said, 'Betty, what are you wearing for the party?' I said, 'Clothes!' and put the receiver down. Her name was Sally.

Not surprisingly, Betty has nothing good to say about Mariella. In 1978 Novotny announced that she had started work on her autobiography, in which she announced that she was going to print names and places. She was found dead in her bed in February 1983. It was claimed by the police that she had died of a drug overdose, although others suspected murder. 'Hah,' spits Betty. 'She drowned in her own vomit!'[8]

Mariella had a daughter by Eddie, who was shunted off to a private school in Switzerland at a very young age. She met Betty's daughter, and the two of Eddie's children became very friendly. Betty feels otherwise: 'I've never met her and I never want to meet her. It was a terribly painful time. My daughter said she was a very nice girl. The entire Mariella story doesn't come up any more. It's ancient history.'

Even when he was in Rome with Mariella, Eddie came and went regularly. He was never away that long. When asked about Eddie's time in Rome with Mariella and whether Betty had boyfriends during the times of separation, she said: 'I've always had a few boyfriends – I never let time slip by!' It can never be emphasised enough that Betty was never a victim to Eddie's wanderings. When they were together, they were together; when apart, Betty lived her own independent and ful-filling life.

It was during the time that Eddie was in Rome with Mariella that Betty became involved with a consultant who was sent up from his main base to work at an industrial facility near Shenley. Decades later he wrote a poignant letter to her reminiscing about their time together. The relationship went on for about a year, and both entered into it knowing that it would eventually come to an end. Although some might label it an affair, it was far deeper and much more personal for both, as evidenced by his letter. He begins by recalling his first arrival at Shenley, as he drives up the lane to the Lodge, and encounters a magnificent Rolls-Royce being washed by an elegant blonde woman in her forties. As he asked her whether accommodation was available – at that time Shenley was still being run as a bed and breakfast – there was an immediate attraction.

He was joined a few days later by a work colleague, and in the eve-nings they would go for the evening meal in the nearby town of St Albans. Within a week or two, he recalls, Betty asked him if he would like to have his evening meal with her in the dining room. During their meal she told him where her private bedroom was, at the end of the first floor, and invited him to knock on her door later that eve-ning when the other guests had turned in for the night. So started an intimate and exquisite relationship that continued throughout his time there. Betty talked to him about Eddie's life and philandering, and showed him all of the bullet holes in the lounge, where Eddie and his cronies would meet and argue.

Late one night when he was in bed with Betty, her maid – who he describes as a simple-minded, uneducated little person – became suspicious about their activities late at night, and knocked on Betty's private room door with some lame questions about food and meals for the next day. So that Betty could talk with her, he had to escape into the bitterly cold bathroom. He remembers sitting on the edge of the bath totally unclothed, for at least 20 minutes while Betty tried to get rid of her! The crude and outmoded furnace for the coal-fired heating system was always causing problems and, after that night, was the first priority on the list of refurbishments as Betty turned Shenley into a health farm.

The kitchen area in the unrefurbished Lodge was also primitive. Somehow, breakfasts and evening meals managed to be prepared. He recalls being in there one evening after Betty had been food shopping at the local supermarket. The same maid was opening the bags of food. At that time, Sainsbury's plastic bags had the logo 'Fresh From Sainsbury's'. As the maid opened one of these bags, either he or Betty asked 'what are those?', to which the maid replied, after looking at the bag, 'they are fresh froms!'

He was there on a day when an episode of *The Avengers* television series was being filmed at the Lodge. A helicopter chase was part of the programme. Luckily for him, he arrived back from where he was consulting just as the filming was over, but the actors and crew were still there. He met Diana Rigg and Patrick Macnee, the principal players. The specially adapted Alouette helicopter was equipped with a stabilised camera platform and was basically a huge bubble cockpit with a skeletal structure behind it. Betty knew he kept a Pentax camera with him, and by fluttering her eyelids and using her provocative charms on the helicopter pilot (he recalls), got him to agree to take the consultant up with him so he could take some overhead pictures of the Lodge, just for Betty. He took off for a 30-minute hovering flight over the Lodge and its grounds while he shot off a roll of film, which he then gave to her.

Betty took him to the local pub where, being close to several film studios, there were often actors to be seen, many of whom knew Betty. He recalls being introduced to Betty and Eddie's long-time friend Burl Ives, and the actor Patrick Magee. He also went with Betty to London's West End and visited Harrods and Fortnum & Mason. Betty bought a superbly styled black coat; when he happened to notice a nice suit, Betty bought it for him despite his protest. Typically of Betty, she said, 'Have it. It's only money.'

Towards the final months of the consultant's time at Shenley, Betty became heavily involved in the making of the film *Triple Cross* and was spending a lot of time in Paris. She would regularly phone him at the Lodge in the evenings and tell him what was going on. He was deeply touched that she cared enough about the friendship they had developed to bother to do this.

It was also during his stay that the conversion of Shenley into a health farm began to take place. It started in the basement – with the antiquated furnace. All the guest rooms were being updated and redecorated as well, and Betty progressively got the other guests to leave. But she insisted that he stayed on while he was still working near there. In the basement, a genuine pinewood Swedish sauna was installed along with three cold-plunge mineral baths. Betty had taken on an expert trainer with whom her friend had a good rapport, and he taught him how to perform forward somersaults using just a left, then just a right arm on its own to start the roll.

The opening of Shenley Lodge health farm was likely to take place before his consulting work was finished and he talked this over with Betty. He was now the only person occupying one of the refurbished rooms, everyone else having departed, and all the other internal work was virtually over. He remarked that he will forever be grateful to Betty for saying to him one night that she wouldn't hold the opening party until his work was over, a matter then of maybe four to six weeks. With the huge investment involved in the project and all the other interested investors involved, he said he would probably never know how 'this amazing woman' arranged this on his behalf. Who else, he wonders – about to embark on such a venture – would have been this thoughtful. On his final Friday morning before leaving for the very last time, he and Betty had coffee together on the balcony overlooking the rear garden. The departure was emotional for both, and he says that his tears were unashamed when finally saying goodbye to this warm, tender, caring, yet determined and resolute woman who had widened his horizons in many ways and changed the course of his life. He said that 'even though we both knew from the start of our friendship that it would be over one day and we both would go our separate ways, it was during these last moments with her that I suddenly realised just what Betty had meant to me during my stay'. Clearly, he had fallen in love with her.

He and his later ex-wife received an invitation to the delayed opening party of the health farm later in 1967. This was the first and only time he met her 'notorious and courageous, yet dubious husband'. He seems to have had no idea that Eddie was there with two mistresses. He remembers that Betty wore an exquisite pink dress and, seeing her again, thoughts of their year-long relationship raced through his mind. He stated that the warmth, elegance, poise and strength of character of this woman were a privilege for him to know.

Later in the 1960s Eddie lived with Betty at Shenley for a while, but at some point he was off again, living with a girl in a flat in the exclusive Barbican in the centre of London:

I remember one day I was coming up to Shenley and in those days I had a Rolls-Royce we had acquired just before he met one of his women. The day before he moved in with her the Rolls was at home, so I said, 'All right. You've got the woman, then I'll have the Rolls.' Yes, I exchanged Eddie for a Rolls-Royce! I had that Rolls for years, it was the twin of one that the Duke of Gloucester had.

About two or three years after I got Shenley I was still driving laundry to the launderette. In those days we still had it as a residential health club but we didn't have the commercial washing machines we had when we had the health farm. Someone once said, 'You're the only lady that drives a Rolls to the launderette!'

I also had a Bentley when I was at Shenley. Somebody had smashed into my Rolls-Royce. It was a diplomat and they couldn't do anything to him so it got written off. Then I got the Bentley and I wouldn't let Eddie drive it to the pub in case he smashed it up. We had such rows about it that I decided to sell it; I sold it to someone in America. The car had already gone and then I received the cheque and it bounced so I never got paid for that, I just lost it! The solicitor said that it would cost more money to fight for it, so we just left it. After Eddie had died I lost all my jewellery too, I sold it to a pawn shop.

A lot of the early days when I was running Shenley, our daughter lived at our flat in London with our nanny. She was old-fashioned and quite scary. Eddie once said: 'There's only one woman I'm afraid of and Jesus, that's your nanny.' She was offered Princess Margaret's children, but she turned them down. Eventually she did go to St James's Palace and worked there for a while, but then she came back to me and came to Shenley.

Eddie was living with a woman just a few streets away and was always tearing about in a little white sports car, with her in a red fox fur hat and blue jeans and him in a beret, trying to recapture his youth. They were absolutely petrified in case Nanny saw them.

Meanwhile, Shenley was continuing to attract an international clientele, and in particular the previously mentioned visitors from the Middle East. Thus, Eddie was unusually well placed to find out what was happening in places where British Intelligence couldn't get agents in. 'I never knew whether he was still providing information when we were at Shenley,' Betty says. 'It's often been asked, "Was he still a spy?" Once a spy, always a spy, I suppose.'

While Eddie was away, he never kept any steady communication with his daughter. Betty says, 'I kept up the communication between him and my daughter. I used to send parcels from him to her and write letters or cards to him from her, and we kept up this pretence for quite a time.'

Of Shenley, Betty says:

Shenley Lodge represented a very demanding time for me both physically and mentally. Everyone who came through the doors had a problem: emotional or otherwise, so you became a counsellor from the word go. I always said anyone could open a health farm, but few people were able to run one successfully because of the many, many and varied demands. I spent many hours of my days talking to people, persuading, cajoling and encouraging, especially very young people from overseas left in our care. Some of them were here for quite serious operations. I went daily to London's Harley Street to visit and comfort one young boy of 14 who came to us.[9] He came to us wearing irons (calipers) and after a severe operation and long convalescence he left for home able to walk without his irons. These successes made the long periods of hard work and anxiety so worthwhile. Parents would come with them and stay for a while, see that they were being cared for, and then just leave them with us. This happened time and time again.

One of my many outstanding although not particularly pleasant memories of Shenley was of a New Year's Eve party for 150 people, with a buffet and a steel band. So much preparation and expense had gone into this. Come the day, it snowed heavily making it impossible to reach us, more so as access to Shenley was by way of a fairly steep, winding narrow road. We had spent days heating the building, the only means being by way of fuel fires – lovely to look at but hell to maintain. Staff for the occasion came in before the snow, and as a result they couldn't get out and visitors couldn't get in – all except a Scotsman, his wife, and a friend who, having paid for the evening, were hell-bent on getting there. They abandoned their car in the local village, hitched up their skirts and trousers, and arrived soaking wet and thoroughly chilled just before midnight. They had the entire party to themselves. It took two days before anyone could get in or out, so ending up an expensive disaster.

One famous actor was a regular with us, since he was doing a lot of filming at the nearby MGM studios. I used to get him his brandy in his morning coffee and drive him to the studio. He used to be in such a state. He was wonderful. He used to sit on the floor and play with my daughter. He loved nothing more than coming back from the studios and playing with her.

The boxer John Conteh used to stay with Eddie and Betty and did a lot of his training at Shenley. Eddie remembers the time:

We trained Johnny Conteh down there. We took him from amateur to until he won the world championship. He loved apple pies and he used to eat them before the fights. Betty used to take them down there for him. Before the fight began we used to shout out

'Apple Pie Johnny, Apple Pie Johnny.' We used to buy ringside seats. At that time he was such a popular guy.

Betty continues the story:

> He was on television after he won the world championship and gave an awful interview. He sat there almost motionless, and when asked 'why do you box', all he had to say was 'for the money'. He was so nervous that was all they got out of him and I thought, 'Oh, Jesus!' Patrick Wymark was sitting there with me watching the interview, so I said to him, 'When he comes back will you please give him a few lessons on what to say and what to do.' Conteh was quite flattered because Pat at that time was number one on the television. Anyway, for about a week we rehearsed with him, and the next time he went on television he got rave reviews from us. John Conteh's girlfriend in the days was a successful writer, and used to come to Shenley regularly as well, always arriving in her blue Rolls-Royce.

'Everyone who came to Shenley wanted to meet Eddie', says Betty. 'I set up the health farm and Eddie organised the exercise.' Lilian Verner-Bonds relates a story about one of Eddie's exercise workouts:

> The local pub called The Fisheries attracted a well-to-do clientele of executives, actors and racing drivers. The men would come to The Fisheries in the afternoon, normally have just a bit too much to drink, and then go on to Shenley. Because they were going home to their wives, Eddie would make them have a sauna and put them through their paces, exercising so that they would then go home okay. I remember one of the racing drivers telling me that a bunch of them had had too much to drink, and that they were going to do the sauna after their exercise workout. He said, 'We were all in the gym, lying on the floor totally drunk, but we knew he would make us do some exercises. Unfortunately, we forgot that that day he was show-ing around a group of very influential people, and they came into the gym. Eddie said to the visitors, "Well, yes, these are my boys",

and Eddie said to us, "Get along boys, straight up the climbing bars", which went up to the ceiling. We climbed painfully to the top with Eddie giving encouragement, and when we were at the top he said, "Okay boys, turn around now and hang from the bars." The racing driver told me that every now and again there was a crash as one by one they fell down onto the floor and just lay there in a heap. 'Eventually I was the only one still hanging on, so as not to let Eddie down. Eddie didn't say a word as we continued to crash to the floor. Eventually he turned to his distinguished visitors, and just said to them, "Boys will be boys." At that point, they left!'

A prominent member of the House of Lords was the subject of another of Eddie's workouts:

He was really a fat and useless individual. He was a completely spoilt brat. He inherited his title when he was 21 along with a vast sum of money. One day he was lifting weights and Eddie said to him, 'Come on ten more.' Suddenly he stopped and said, 'I hate you, I hate you, I hate you.' 'Good,' Eddie said. 'At least you can hate now. You couldn't hate anyone when you came here.'

Mrs Verner-Bonds knew Eddie and Betty through many of their years at Shenley and after, and also had a lot to say about the relationship between them. 'Betty was very strong,' she says. 'And Eddie always talked about her.' Despite his affairs with other women, he always came back. 'She was his rock. That was the sad thing for the women he went off with,' Lilian says. 'Eddie could never break that bond with Betty.'

Betty agrees. 'Eddie always said, "Never resist temptation".' He never did. Verner-Bonds tells another story related to her by Betty:

Once when he was back at Shenley, Eddie woke up around 3 a.m. in a panic. 'Bloody hell!' he shouted, stumbling around in the darkness, trying to find his clothes. 'I've got to get home! I've got to get home!' At which point Betty sat up and gently said: 'Eddie, you *are* bloody well home.'

Others have stories about Eddie's time at Shenley. 'On the occasion of my first visit I arrived at the impressive front entrance of Shenley, only to hear the most fearsome of noises from the roof of the mansion. It was on this roof I met Eddie strapped into a Vickers machine gun – firing at a sheet draped between two oak trees half a mile away.' Told about anyone else, the story would stretch credulity – but not when it is told about Eddie.

It was during this period that Betty first became interested in the psychic world. It would have an influence on her later life, particularly after Eddie's passing. And, the success that Betty was making of Shenley, along with Eddie's intermittent but important input, led her to another of the major episodes in her life: Kilkea Castle.

MY HOME IS
MY (IRISH) CASTLE

Fully aware of the success that Betty was making of Shenley, in 1971 the Irish government contacted her with a view to her taking on an ancient castle. She recalls:

I got a call from the Irish tourist board to ask me if I would take an interest in an old castle. They wanted a health farm to be built in Kildare, Ireland and wanted me to advise them on it. They already had Kilkea Castle in mind. We had lots of discussions and then I went over and met the man who was running the castle at the time, Doctor Bill Cade, to make arrangements to join him in partnership. He was an interesting man, in the travel business. He knew everybody in the business, which was great for the castle. I thought it sounded exciting, and I already had a lot of contact with Ireland because of our previous shipping business. I'd been friendly for many, many years with Kathleen Ryan who was a famous Irish actress. She was married to the most handsome surgeon. I often think about them, because Eddie fell in love with her, and I fell in love with her husband. We were good friends for years. I used to stay at her family home, Burton Hall, on the outskirts of Dublin.

Dr Cade was a good friend to have, except that he was keen about me and that made it very difficult. I did like him as well, he was an extremely handsome man, very tall, but it was awkward. Cade used to promote as well, and he used to do my entire itinerary. In the end I bought the castle. He sold his shares to me and I already had the rest, so I ended up owning the whole thing, and he stayed on in a consultancy capacity. I was the chairperson and managing director. There was a lot of jealousy because an English Protestant woman running such an organisation in Catholic Ireland was really quite something. Because of this, almost from the first day, the IRA was a problem.

Kilkea Castle is the oldest inhabited castle in Ireland. It was built in 1180 by Hugh de Lacy, chief governor of Ireland, for the warrior Walter de Riddlesford, eleven years after the Anglo-Norman invasion of the country. From 1244 Kilkea Castle was in the possession of the Fitzgeralds, one of the greatest Irish families, destined to produce the late President of the United States, John Fitzgerald Kennedy. Betty was introduced to a person connected to President Kennedy with a view to Kennedy's wife coming over for the opening of the castle, but with security issues it became impractical.

The name Kilkea is a corruption of the Gaelic *Cill Caoide*, meaning St Caoide, who was a disciple of St Patrick. The castle was a place of refuge for the many centuries of Ireland's bloody history. In the original tower is found a haunted room, where the 11th Earl of Kildare, the 'Wizard Earl', practised the 'Black Arts' in the sixteenth century. Betty adds: 'We even had our own haunted rooms.'

When it first went on the market years and years before, the workmen were sent in to demolish parts of the castle. They went to this one particular area and started to smash the walls. As they opened a sealed room, there was a woman sitting in a chair and she disintegrated in the air. The story goes that when the Earl of Kildaire lived there, this was his lady. The Earl went out hunting and he came back and found that his estate manager had been sleeping with his wife. He had her bricked up in a room and left her there to die as punishment, and her ghost is still there now. No one ever used that room, it was locked up. There's also another haunted room at the top of the castle. Things were always appearing there. I was told never to go up there. Naturally I was itching to get there. One day I gave in and went up. It was a little room right at the top at the back of the castle and it just had a bed in it. It didn't make any great impact on me when I went into it. Apparently people over the years had kept an eye on it because all sorts of things had been found there, like excrement on the bed, dead birds, with no evidence of where it had come from – the room was kept permanently locked.

When Betty arrived to take charge, the castle was already in use as a hotel – old, interesting, but not very modern. Her experience with Shenley had taught her that to attract top guests and functions, the place had to be of a very high standard. This was far from the case. Even the tables in the dining room were still bare wood. But, there was a complication: the castle was a listed building, a building of historic interest and protected by the government. To shift a single stone required consent. Betty recalls:

I built a function hall for 350 people and 2,800ft² of health farm adjacent to the castle, and it was very hard to do because this was a listed building. You had to have special permission and you had to use special materials, complying with a great number of rules. At the beginning of all of this the inspectors were terrified that if I put a foot wrong the place would fall down. In the end, I altered the place a lot. They nearly died when I took down walls to build archways and new facilities. When I built the Function Hall it had to be built of the same stone as the castle, in keeping with its status as a listed building. I actually got coloured leaded windows to match the castle's to put in the Function Hall, and they had to be the finest there was in Ireland. I also built another house called The River House, which had twenty rooms, to use as overflow when we had overseas visitors. One of these visitors was the American boxer Muhammad Ali, who stayed with us while he was there for a bout in Ireland. The boxers Frank Bruno[1] and John Conteh also used to train there before their big bouts.

The health farm itself had separate facilities for men and women, built as a modern extension on the castle. I went to Germany for the basic equipment, and I did a tour all over the place: I went to France, Germany, Italy, America and Switzerland to get the latest in everything for the rest of the modernisation. It was, for a time, the only health club in the country.

Realising that the dining room was in many ways the heart of the experience for guests, Betty set about transforming it from what she describes as 'a common cafe' into an elegant dining experience, in keeping with the clientele she intended to attract. She had a special rug woven, incorporating the castle's crest; she covered the walls with French grey rice paper, a special paper like linen, dark grey with overtones of red. She added beautiful silverware and stylish tablecloths, and had handsome new chairs made. Overhead were glittering chandeliers. She marvellously understates: 'It was quite a transformation.' The chairman of the H.J. Heinz Company and his family were very supportive and were regular visitors. They said to Betty that it had to be the most gracious dining room in the whole of Ireland. There was also a ballroom that got Betty's special touch. There had been a sprung floor installed at some time in the past, but it was badly scratched, and the perimeter was a mass of cigarette burns: it was typical of the state that the castle had lapsed into.

In addition to massive refurbishment, she also added a new bar inside the castle, the Cavalier Bar, which was a very smart cocktail bar. For the local people, she built the Kitchen Bar. This was an entirely new experience for them and it met with universal approval. The first Christmas she was there she decided to do the same thing that she did at Shenley, which was to give everyone a Christmas present. There was over sixty staff, so it was quite a task. She arranged a special afternoon so that she could distribute the presents: the staff, who were absolutely gobsmacked, said they had never been treated so well before.

We sold souvenirs of the castle as well. I found lots of historical pictures of it and had them reproduced. I had biscuits made by biscuit manufacturers and I had souvenir tins made with a picture of the castle on the top and all the famous castles in Ireland all around the side.

Some improvements had unexpected consequences:

The Australian Ambassador, there for a conference, said he would like to look over the castle, so I showed him around. We had a beautiful ladies toilet, which was done out in French style. I took him in, for a joke, and I said, 'Now this is for the ladies, really', and afterwards he said to me, 'You know, Mrs Chapman, I always judge a hotel by its toilet facilities.' Who would have thought it!

The improvements were not limited to 'downstairs'. All of the fifty or so rooms were renovated, and en suite bathrooms were installed. At the time, this was a rarity in Ireland, and was a rarity even in some London hotels of the time. Even so, of all the refurbishments and upgrades, Betty remarked: '1180 AD was a pretty hard act to follow!'

The refurbishments were hardly without problems:

They were bringing in heavy equipment one day, huge equipment, but they had laid the floors and had forgotten to put in the services for the equipment. Another day they had hung the doors into the kitchen and they had not brought in the large kitchen equipment. How did they think they were going to get it in? I was always on site for some problem. I knew a lot about building contractors. I was lucky that during my Brighton period I had to do contract building there, so I was pretty quick to suss out if it wasn't going right. There were endless problems. Because I was English and because of the IRA, everything always seemed to be difficult. I think it was really resentment. I was both chairperson and managing director of the castle. I did my best to fit in with the local community. Even though I was Church of England, I still went to Catholic services with many of the staff. It was politics rearing its ugly head yet again. When we had our monthly meetings we all sat at this long table with all of the accountants and senior staff and so on. I always sat at the head of the table as chairperson, but I could see that there were one or two of them who really resented it.[2]

When we were fully open, it was all a great success. We had masses of functions there; people came from all over the world. But, there was always a fine line to tread. For example, one day my manager came running in to me shouting: 'Are you crazy. Get that flag down!' We always used to fly the flag of the country whose group we were hosting, and I used to have flowers on the table in the colours of the country to make it special for them. In this case it was an Australian group, and the Australian Ambassador was coming for lunch. The Australian flag has a Union Jack in the corner, a hated symbol in much of Ireland. I was warned that the flag, and possibly even more of the castle, would be blown up if I didn't get it down.

Despite the problems due to my being English and Protestant, we had the first All-Ireland Peace Conference in the castle. They were there for three days – the North and the South. I was sent home, the organisers did not think it was wise to have me there. They ringed the place with steel for security. The conference didn't do any good, but it was the first that took place.

There was always promotion going on for the castle and its facilities. Betty did a long promotional tour in Europe. As she recently remarked:

I was looking at the itinerary yesterday and it was quite an exhausting tour. Then I went to America to try to persuade the more upmarket tourists to come, particularly since by this time it had a health farm, and the Function Hall. The night before the American agents came, I was talking to them in New York and they said 'Now is it safe?', and I said, 'Of course it is safe, it is only the newspapers which give out these scary stories.'

As often happened with Betty's luck, just a few days afterwards several people were killed in the main street in Dublin.

I used to go back and forth every couple of weeks between the castle and Shenley. Evelyn Black, my friend, was running Shenley with Eddie, whilst I was in Ireland. Evelyn Black was one of the best things that ever happened to me. She was with us for twenty-seven years, and remains a good friend to this day. In fact, she really remains part of our family. I enjoyed my five years at Kilkea Castle, it was an interesting project. I travelled a lot to promote it, for one month in Europe alone, France, Germany, Italy, Portugal and plenty more. I was alone and it was hard work. I had to get as much knowledge as I could about how I could liaise with different countries regarding the health farm. It was a really busy place with lots of travel agents involved. I had forty-five permanent staff in the castle and sixty for big events. I lived in the castle; I had a general manager who made me a lovely suite, after having just a room and a bathroom originally. My suite was called the 'Esmeralda Suite'. Eddie came to stay and brought friends with him.

My assistant was extremely useful, since he could see things that other people couldn't or wouldn't. He would put a watch on the Function Hall kitchen and at 1.30 a.m. the chef was sitting outside and half pissed. The women staff were going home with big bags of food that they had stashed outside the back door. Even the general manager had a huge deep freeze full of everything. It was yet another burden when I was new to it and trying to build up and run the place at the same time. Needless to say, it all stopped very abruptly.

The first general manager lived in the lodge at the end of the drive and then after he left in disgrace I had another one who actually lived in the castle, so I moved out of my personal sitting room downstairs to a double room and bathroom upstairs so he could have living quarters for himself, convenient to the workings of the castle. I must say he did himself proud. It was a popular move with the staff, because I was English and no one expected anyone English to do any such thing.

The new general manager ran a very tight ship for me. If he heard that anyone had done anything to upset me, he had them carpeted at once. Another time we had someone special coming and the house-keeper Kate Nelligan was complaining about the condition of the stairs – that they weren't up to scratch. On examining the stairs I found that they really were not satisfactory. I was a bit fussy about it all, so I decided that I would scrub the stairs myself, and say 'this is the way it should be'. I also wanted them to know that I was not averse to getting down on my hands and knees and doing things myself. The staff were all quite amused, but they got the message!

Kate always used to warn me about coming downstairs in late hours. She was aware of some of the shenanigans that the staff got up to. One night I had a restless night, and wanted a cup of tea. I decided to come down to the kitchen and make it myself rather than disturb the night porter. So I just tumbled down in my nightie and my rollers expecting that there would be no one around at that late hour. And to my enormous surprise there were about twenty of the staff having a bean feast. They were as surprised as I was. I said, 'Oh, excuse me', and I left. The next day I discussed it with Nellie and she said, 'Oh, I warned them.' I decided not to make a fuss about it because they were good staff and I had good relations with them. They worked very well for me and for long hours, so I decided it was nothing to make a fuss about.

During the summer, the gardens were open to the public because we had beautiful gardens. These gardens stretched right down to the River Breeze, which was filled with trout. There were very interesting objects in the garden, as well as beautifully laid out plants. One of these objects was a centuries-old Tithe Table, which was stolen.[3] There was a great deal of publicity across Ireland about this, and it was eventually recovered.

Betty had an extremely unpleasant experience in the same garden:

I was sat in the garden one day, and the housekeeper came with a tray of tea for me and some guests. I happened to move and the whole tray of tea fell in my lap. I had to go to hospital and have all my burns and blisters syringed because they were so large. I was in pain for a very long time afterwards. It was horrible. I missed walking in those beautiful gardens when I left.

There was a lot of impromptu entertainment, much of which took place in the garden when weather permitted. 'If there were passing dancers or singers or something they would ask if they could play at the castle. We would take up a collection for them, and some of the talent was great – a lot of Irish folk dancing, and really good music.'

Despite problems arising almost immediately with the IRA, her relationship with people in the area was very good:

Despite being hated by many for being English, many of our Irish staff were as nice as could be, and despite problems with the IRA, not all of them were full of hostility either. There was a major in the IRA who was stationed nearby. He would turn up and we always had a sing-song. The local people were decent too, because whenever there was any IRA activity in the area we would be forewarned.

Even so, one night we had about 250 people in the hotel and about an equal number in the function suite. We suddenly had a call to say that bombs had been placed all over the castle. And being an old building, there were very many places that they could be hidden. So I got out of my bed, and I had to clear the hotel. We had a big white horse called Bony, and my driver Jim got on this horse and got a megaphone and called everyone out of the hotel, and of course they had to disperse into the grounds. Imagine 500 people in the early hours of the morning. They spread out all over the castle grounds right down to the river. The police searched the place, but it so happened that it was a hoax and they finally found the man who made the phone call. All he got was three months. I mean, all the aggravation. People who came to the hotel were from all over the world and you can imagine how things like this affected business, so you were always fighting. I once found an advert which was placed in the local paper in Northern Ireland for people to come to the

143

castle for peace and quiet after the Troubles in the North. Someone sent in a letter and pinned the advert to it, making some vile comment, and saying, 'Stick your castle up your arse.'

The same night as the hoax bomb-threat, one of our Filipino staff was coming across the bridge over the river near the Function Hall, and she said she had heard the cry of the banshee. She was so scared, she said, that the hairs stood up on her arms. It is said that if you hear the cry of the banshee someone dies within three days. The next day, one of our neighbours died.

The Filipino who heard the banshee was a relative of one of the Filipinos who worked for me at Shenley. The Filipinos were fantastic, and good workers. The castle and its environs had 101 acres of land, including our own church. I always went to the Catholic Church with the staff. I was used to the Catholic Church from my visits to Katherine Ryan's family at Bunton Hall, outside Dublin. Katherine's mother turned everyone out of bed at an early hour, regardless of their religion, to attend Mass. Many times the guests were nursing hangovers.

In addition to our permanent staff, most of the local villagers were on standby in case we had large functions. When the group Human Potential came from America there were over 350 of them, which was more than we had capacity for in the castle. That is why we built the River House, otherwise the overflow had to be accommodated in the village. We had our own chef for the conference hall, which could easily accommodate 300 people. We had our own sous-chef for the castle. The castle was always so busy, but it had its own kitchens, because I also built new kitchens for the castle. I was on my feet constantly, the whole time I was there, not the least of which was because it was 100 steps up to my bedroom. My general manager said that it was unsustainable for me to have to run up and down the stairs every time I wanted to rest, which is why he had the suite made for me so I could rest there whenever I wanted, or on the rare occasions I entertained there. John and Kitty Mills were great friends of ours and they were frequent visitors there.[4] Richard Burton was one of those who frequently joined us.

Another visitor of note to Kilkea was Princess Helena Moutafian, MBE, a name scarcely known to the public at the time, but the recipient of a large number of civic awards in Britain, France and Russia for her charitable and social works. The daughter of the Russian prince Alexei Gagarin, she, along with Dame Barbara Cartland, were close friends of Betty.[5]

In addition to the functions at the castle itself, it was also necessary to set up outside activities such as fishing and riding:

I even started a football team for the castle, and another for the jockeys from the local Jockey Club, who trained there. I gave them a piece of land for their own football club. The football pitch where the local football team played belonged to the castle. I had built facilities for them on that land. At the time that I was forced into bankruptcy on a technicality and lost the castle, I wanted to leave something behind, so I backdated the sale of the football ground to the village team, so that they would have it perpetually. I should think there are still football teams there now.

I was quite proud of what I did there; the entire thing was a huge project. But once again I got robbed of it. Banks and accountants, once again, took me to the cleaners – after I had modernised the castle and made it a going concern. They forced me into bankruptcy on a technical point, because they tried to make me prove that I had enough money to support Kilkea all the time, which I didn't. I didn't want to lose Shenley Lodge. God knows I'd given up five years of my life, and many people have run very successful businesses without much money at hand – the money comes after. But they took Kilkea away from me.

The day I found out I was at Shenley. I nearly collapsed, and I couldn't believe it, that after giving so much of my life, people could be so awful. The world is full of ungrateful, ungracious people. I didn't even go back; I have never been back, even though one day now I would love to. All of my stuff was packed up and sent to me.

It remained open as a health farm. Betty reflects:

When you're dealing with governments or politicians, someone sometimes happens not to like you because you had some tussles with them. I did a lot for the Irish tourist business. I was really bitter because I had neglected Shenley. I had five long years of grind. My personal assistant from the castle later wrote to me: 'You know, Betty, when you left Kilkea, all the locals said that all the graciousness went out of it.'

11

A HEALTHY BUSINESS

Betty had developed Shenley Lodge in a way that hadn't been tried before in Europe. As a consequence, she became an expert in the field of health clubs. She developed a highly satisfactory formula for the organisation and management of a health resort. Shenley was like a master plan; everybody wanted one like it. Betty had numerous connections with royals and all sorts of other people who had visited Shenley. Because of this, various prominent people wanted her to set up health farms for them. One such visitor was the Shah of Iran,[1] who also persuaded King Hussein's sister, Princess Basma,[2] to stay at Shenley. Ironically, one of their last clients, one recommended by the Shah, became Eddie's last mistress. But in the years immediately before Betty's involvement in Iran, other countries beckoned. Unfortunately, it turned into a time of massive disappointment for her:

I visited Nigeria in 1976 because one of my clients at Shenley Lodge was the wife of a banker, and she wanted me to build a health farm similar to Shenley in Nigeria, on the central Jos Plateau, which consisted of extensive lava surfaces dotted with many extinct volcanoes. It was almost like an English getaway in Nigeria, for the British that worked there.

The idea was that I would set up a main building like I had done at Shenley, which had treatments, saunas, shops and everything to do with the health farm. But instead of having bedrooms like we had at Kilkea Castle, accommodation would be in twenty-five chalets, which I would also build. A friend of mine called Sue, whose husband was a lawyer, prepared a business plan for me. It was financed by the husband of the lady that stayed at Shenley and originally approached me about it. It had a budget of about £3 million. In Nigeria, I first went to her home on Victoria Island; then to a big hotel like the Hilton, where we met and discussed the plan.

It was a vast undertaking, I worked on it for about three years, coming and going by Scottish Airlines to Nigeria. Sometimes I would stay with the banker and his wife and at other times in the hotel. We would then take a plane together to the area where the work was. The idea was that I would train all the staff at Shenley and then send them to Nigeria to run the place. I had planning permission, and everything to do with the project. It was ready to go.

But sadly, the banking facilities fell apart – her husband suddenly left the bank (I suspected skulduggery). So, the £3 million was gone, and the plans were all scrapped. All the same, my friend, who arranged it all, still came to Shenley for the years to come. She was a little greedy and rather than let me get on with the chalets and furnish them, she wanted to do it so that she could make the profit. I think she was responsible for the downfall as she took too much out of it. She would come to England and buy stuff which she would then sell on for a lot more in Nigeria. She had a good relationship with customs and got away with a lot! In fairness, I must say that I was taken very good care of. I had everything that it was possible to have, and I was spoiled rotten by everyone I met there. The Nigerians themselves were nice and so I couldn't complain.

At around the same time, the Turkish government invited me to do the same there. They wanted to buy an apartment block in

Larnaca, in Turkish Cyprus, and asked if I would set up an operation there. So, I got on with all the arrangements for that. It was all laid out and they got the building. We had arranged our terms which, as with the Nigerian project, were for Shenley training for staff, for me to take care of the whole thing. But then they demanded that I commit myself to them for twenty-five or thirty years, to take care of them (and show them a nice profit). I thought that was too much of a burden, because I had my own responsibilities at Shenley. So, in the end, the project was abandoned.

Then, I went to Kuwait to do a similar project for the Emir. The Emir was taken care of by a doctor friend that we knew in England. He was going to finance the setting up of a health clinic in Kuwait. That's where I experienced my first sandstorm – it blew me away. Setting up the project was a very tricky thing to do because men and women couldn't be seen together, so I had to have different places for each. Therefore, it meant a lot of planning and work. So, I arranged my fee and everything for that, which I believe was going to cost a couple of million. His physician was in overall charge of the project on the Emirate's behalf. What happened? With my luck, as always, the Emir died – and with him, the project.

I was also invited to set up an operation in the Philippines. There was a surgeon there who performed psychic operations, so we had correspondence. His people used to come over here and talk to me about it, and there were great, great discussions again. I thought that it was quite exciting. The idea was to set up a clinic with a health farm attached for after-surgery care. And, of course, that fell through. It was just too far away for me to operate something like that. Not only that, it was a time of great unrest in the Philippines, around the time of the overthrow of President Marcos.

The Shah of Iran's sister, Princess Shahnaz invited me to Iran in 1978.[3] She wanted me to build a health farm in her home area of Shiraz. I knew the rest of the family already, because the Shah's family used to stay at Shenley. On the way to Tehran I stayed in Kuwait with an English friend, John Fox and his wife. He was always dealing in something with the Arab world. He had sold some cement to the Iraqis – this happened while I was there – and he'd obviously done the 'best' deal that he could. That was his style. He got a message while I was there from the Iraqis saying, in so many words, that he'd ripped them off. And they said, 'If you don't return the money we will send someone out to remove your private parts.' So, without any hesitation, he agreed. Not only did he lose his profit, he lost the money that he'd invested in the cement. Eventually he came back to England, and years later I went to his funeral to see him off!

When I got to Tehran from Kuwait, the press was there waiting for me in the early hours of the morning, as Eddie's film (*Triple Cross*) had been shown there recently. Eddie never actually came with me to Iran but the Shah's family was very fond of him and loved to be entertained by him at Shenley. I went to Iran to stay with Parri Wyatt, whose husband was the ambassador to Jordan. Parri was the equivalent of a lady-in-waiting to Princess Manijeh, the Shah's niece. It was through them that I met Princess Basma, who frequently came to Shenley and who has also remained a friend. When in Iran, I stayed in Parri's hotel, a very big hotel in the centre of Tehran. All the staff from the airlines used to stay there, and I stayed there on and off for two or three weeks at a time for a year or two. She also owned the Austrian embassy building in Tehran, and several other properties. She was quite well known at that time. On that particular morning, I was late arriving from Kuwait, so we sat in the garden next to the swimming pool having our breakfast and a good long chinwag at five in the morning. It was ever so romantic, I thought. Once, in Kuwait, I got caught in a sandstorm on my way back to Tehran. If you have never been caught in a sandstorm you can't imagine how it is! It is in your ears, your eyes, your clothes, anywhere it can get!

When I first met Princess Shahnaz it was in her palace. I was driven out of the city in a Rolls-Royce up this very wide dual carriageway: I have never seen such a well-kept carriageway! I was escorted by outriders as if I was royalty myself. When we arrived, Princess Manijeh and her husband led the way and we met the secretary of the Iranian Embassy in London. He exclaimed, 'Mrs Chapman!' and greeted me as an old friend. He used to come down to stay with us at Shenley and bring official guests of the embassy. We put our feet up and servants washed the soles of our feet, as is the tradition. I became close friends with Princess Manijeh, who I am still in contact with today; she now lives in Paris. I was even in Tehran one time when it was Princess Manijeh's birthday, and I was the only one at the party not from the family.

Princess Shahnaz was sitting in the middle of a garden, a kind of terrace with a lot of steps. She was sitting in a big high-backed chair, wearing black with jewels stitched all over the dress, and white fox furs draped around her. She was stunning. She was wearing enough jewellery to send me around the world: earrings, bracelets, rings, you can't imagine how many diamonds. Someone told me that at some stage her rings and bracelets were sold in Switzerland for £11 million. After I greeted her, I took my leave of her, but like the Queen here, you mustn't turn your back. So, as I backed away, in doing so, I fell over a rose bush in the garden! It was so embarrassing, with everybody rushing to my aid!

Running right through the middle of the garden going down from the terrace were steps down to a canal at the bottom of the terrace. The steps were made of glass lit from below and with water running underneath, and either side of the steps were steps of flowers. At the bottom of the steps, a canal flowed; there were white swans and black swans. I'd never seen black swans before and I've never seen them since. It was such a picture; I can still see it all if I close my eyes.

I'll remember forever the party that they gave for me in Princess Shahnaz's palace. They cut my hair, and I was dressed in a beautiful costume. When we arrived at the palace we put our feet up and had the soles of our feet cleaned. At the door we were again met by the secretary of the Iranian Embassy in London. The party was given for what I had done for the Shah's family when they stayed with me at Shenley. The palace was built on the top of her beautiful terraced gardens. It had a beautiful dome all in stained glass, like the windows in churches. The dome cost over a million alone.

The tables under the dome were laid out for a feast for two or three hundred, and all lined up along the walls were about twenty chefs all dressed up in their chef's outfits. All of the furniture was iron. There were trees and shrubs in pots all among the tables and around the walls. There were birds in cages and birds in the trees, all singing and twittering. In the middle of the meal, suddenly there was water dropping on me: the hugely expensive roof was leaking, which I found very funny! Afterwards they brought a violinist from Spain to entertain us, and the Shah and the Empress were sitting down in front. I sat with the family but, as we sat in the very big and comfortable armchairs, I fell asleep!

I had arranged to go on a trip with Princess Manijeh, since she was going on an official tour. But her father was taken sick and we couldn't do the tour together as we planned, so I went alone. I went to Qom, where I went to a mosque.[4] There was a particular shrine there and I went to pray. I was going there to pray for someone who was very ill in England. Inside there was a heart-shaped locket and it was full of money and jewels – because people had to donate when they prayed. The people in England had asked me to go there to pray, because they knew that from the time I was on my feet I was down on my knees in prayer! I started lighting candles many years ago, and I light one every day for the planet.

When I went on my journey to Isfahan, I was looked after by the army, who kindly made sure that I saw what I wanted to see. It was a very interesting time. I went to the famous mosque and prayed for people that I knew. It was a really beautiful city. I stayed in the Shah's summer palace with its wide and extensive gardens. When I arrived there were two fellows carrying armchairs and I jokingly said to the courier who had brought me there, 'Oh, are they moving out?' She said, 'That's for you to sit under the trees and have a cool drink.' They brought them from the officers' mess because, although the army looked after me, I was looked after by everybody really. We sat under a tree facing the summer palace. My clearest memory is of the weeping willows; it is such a clear picture to me even today. After our refreshments, we went into the palace, where there were rooms showing all the different countries of the world that had given presents to the Shah. Then I saw the Peacock Throne itself – mind boggling.[5]

All of my plans were well under way when the revolution came along, and the Shah was deposed. The secret police were the Shah's downfall. He was surrounded by people who told him only what he wanted to hear. Empress Farah Dibah was his backbone towards the end, and a timeless worker for the country. There was a massive amount of construction work in Tehran and the bazaar was full of intrigue. But rulers are only successful when surrounded by a trusted team, which they seldom are. Money or positions of power motivate most people when attracted to a new leader or situation. I saw that with Kwame Nkrumah as well.

I didn't go back and all the plans for that part of the world came to an end. I remember one day, around that time, two people drove into Shenley who I thought were from the Iranian Embassy. This day we had visitors from the Shah's family, Princess Manijeh and her husband. On that same day, the Shah's mother and brother were also there, and they were in the lounge having tea. These two people who had just driven up asked for two members of the Shah's family who were there. Their bodyguard, who was standing in the hall, took over immediately. When he became involved, the two people left, and we were never sure whether they were just trying to get at the Shah's family.

Parri's hotel was burnt to the ground, but she went back. She was very brave to do so. She went to claim the ashes, as it were, of the hotel and whatever she had left. She went back and settled into the life that was expected of her, and the contrast from the life she had is amazing.

Parri eventually got back her property in Iran. She had a network of very able supporters, and if she couldn't deal with the Mullahs, then no one could. She was very tough, and very well able to deal with anything and anyone that came her way. She wound up running a travel agency.

'Well, all right,' I thought. 'All of this has blown up in my face, but I still have Shenley … or so I thought.'

12

EDDIE'S LAST BATTLE

Towards the end of the 1980s Betty decided for a number of reasons to retire from the health farm. She decided to sell up and invest in some other business. However, the decline in the property market meant that this was difficult. The building was valued at £1 million. In 1991 she agreed a sale to a Mr Landau, who contracted it on to his company. He opened a school in the building. He failed to complete one year later and, after litigation, and on the insistence of banks involved in the financing, Betty transferred the property to the school and took security over the assets. In 1993, amid great controversy, the bank appointed receivers and sold the property and business for just sufficient money to discharge the debt to the banks, leaving nothing for Betty. The property had been taken from her without a penny being paid. Betty tells the story:

Each time, whenever I went somewhere, something seemed to come along and negate it. When I thought about what happened to all the other ventures, I never thought about anything happening to Shenley. When I bought Shenley, at the time I bought it, it was a good proposition. I got the money and look what I sold it for, even though I didn't get paid. I had the right track and ideas to go on, but alas.

My last client at Shenley was Colonel Gaddafi of Libya's lady friend, a member of the von Trapp family. And as Shenley was closing, the manservant of Suzie von Trapp told me how much Suzie wanted to stay at Shenley; Gaddafi had recommended it to her. I said that she couldn't because we were closing. Anyhow, she pleaded so much that I decided I would take her. She and Eddie became very close when she came, they used to sit on her bed together and talk for hours and hours and hours. She was very small and very pretty, and she came to recuperate after she had a nose job done. Goodness knows why, as she was perfect already. She was very interesting and would always send for us, her 'special friends' whenever she had a cocktail party in London.

Finally, I'd had enough of Shenley; my family thought that I best have a break from the business. Shenley Lodge represented a very demanding time for me, both physically and mentally. Finally, I decided to sell Shenley, with an agent's help. A friend of the agent, a headmaster of a school, said that he would help me as he wanted to be involved in it. It was his idea to build a school there. They worked out that it would be very profitable to keep it rather than sell it on. I would live there and make money but not take any part in running it. I was happy with that. It took about eighteen months for a school to be built inside. They would come and present to me the various things that they were doing. I was involved in many ways with all of it as I had to get permission for it to be changed into a school. The school was to be called Manor Lodge School, as it still is today, a private school, with a few boarders. We built a computer room and it was called The Chapman Computer Room. The mayor of St Albans came and laid the foundation stone for the school. It was a nice school, a uniform school. I was actually living on the premises, in my own quarters, when the kids arrived for the school. I took part in their fetes and took an interest in all they did. They were aged from

11 to 16. I think they liked me because I took part. They knew I'd had a long history with Shenley. I also got on well with the teachers.

When the agent hadn't completed the sale in 1992, I commenced litigation against them as I hadn't seen any money. Lots of banks were involved. It was supposed to be sold for £1 million but I never got the money. The parents took over Shenley and ran it as a charity. Those million pounds got swallowed up somewhere and I have never seen a penny since. There was a lot of bribery between the banks and the lawyers. One bank bribed the man who bought it from me, who hadn't paid me, but he was selling it on. They said that if he would agree to give up fighting with the bank, the case would be dropped. It was a very long, complicated legal process, but the result of it is that I lost everything.

In the end the man that bought it agreed to make a confession that he and the bank were in league together. He confessed to my accountants. Whilst the process was going on, I was given £1,000 a month to get myself somewhere to live. The bank gave a letter of promise to me around October deferring to the following April. The bank asked my agent not to join me in an action against them, so he dropped it, leaving me high and dry. At the time when the case to settle Shenley Lodge was heard, an illegal staff member of the company that represented me in the sale of Shenley was at a hearing in the court. A friend of mine who had just come into my life, Carol Bell, came with me to the hearing, and had a conversation with a lady sitting behind us in the court. She told Carol that a senior member of the company had told her to mess me around because at my age, with luck, 'I would die and the case would die with me.'

After all of the legal shenanigans Betty received a final slap in the face. After the buyout of the school by the parents and teachers, which left Betty out in the cold and penniless, the school held a party to celebrate its 'rescue'. A newspaper reported:

While celebrations are being held at a Shenley school saved from closure, the pensioner who lost the £725,000 she invested in it lies ill in bed. Her accountant, who spoke to *The Times* on her behalf, said she has become ill through the stress of the past few weeks.[1]

Betty also lost the £1 million of the actual sale price.

In 1991, as the Shenley upheaval was still going on, Eddie went to live in the Canary Islands. Betty says:

My son-in-law bought a house there. Eddie wasn't well because of his injured spine, so he went to stay there to recuperate in a holiday home that had been rented for us. I frequently went out to stay, but I had to continue taking care of the Shenley situation. The Canary Islands are really beautiful, and my daughter and my son-in-law had a lovely house there. Eddie stayed there alone for some time. By this time they had four children, and I was a very proud grandmother. I have to say that they were incredibly good children with me. My daughter would sometimes go away and I would take care of the children. They would all go on holiday to their house in the Canary Islands.

When they lived in England afterwards, they had a helicopter for a short period. My son-in-law used to come along in it on a Sunday morning and we'd pootle off for coffee or lunch somewhere, like Devon. One day we had taken off from somewhere and I heard, 'Hold on to Grandma!' The door had flown open, so my grandchildren held onto me.

In one of life's strange coincidences, a Norwegian woman who lived in a flat next door to Eddie's Canary Island lodging got into conversation with him one day. As they were speaking, they realised that they both knew Dagmar Lahlum, his Norwegian wartime girlfriend. Eddie made contact with Dagmar, and they entered into a polite correspondence. It was later revealed that Dagmar had suffered greatly from ostracising after the war for 'collaborating' with the Germans. One writer on Eddie's life seemed to suggest that this was largely down to Eddie not making it plain to the woman's accusers that he was a British agent all along. For unknown reasons of her own, Dagmar never revealed to them that she was with the Norwegian Resistance the whole time – as she revealed to Eddie when they were together.

The Canaries was where a BBC documentary about Eddie was filmed, finally shown in 2012. In it he is shown driving a sports car provided by the BBC (a fact that was not mentioned in the televised documentary), and which appears to show him living in luxury. Nothing could be further from the truth. With Shenley tied up in legal wrangling, Eddie's subsistence in the Canaries was provided by his daughter and son-in-law. Betty recalls:

After Shenley, first we lived in Radlett (about 10 miles from Shenley) and we moved around from place to place, until I settled in Chesham (about 25 miles north-west of London) when Eddie was taken very ill. I missed Shenley because I had spent a huge portion of time there – about thirty years. Eddie became progressively frail and couldn't walk. He ended up in a nursing home.

The loss of Shenley and the obliteration of all they had worked for hit Eddie very hard. His health began a noticeable decline, as Betty remembers: 'He would come down the stairs at night and sit quietly, obviously confused. "Why on earth are they keeping me in this prison? Why?" He thought he was back in prison in Jersey.'

Eventually Betty, ageing herself and suffering from the loss of Shenley as well, was forced to get Eddie into a nursing home:

He suffered greatly from neglect in the nursing home where he spent most of his final years. The worst experience of my whole life was spending weeks at the Lattimer Wing in Amersham for elderly persons. I have never seen such indifference to people's needs, amounting to cruelty. I considered that he was totally neglected. His room was filthy, not having been cleaned since he went there. When I arrived one Sunday he was covered with a filthy wet towel soaked in soup, and when we said we required a dry one, we were told to wait. He was also sitting on a wet cushion, obviously not able to go to the toilet. Another day I went there to find him saturated in urine. It's not surprising since every time he needed to go to the toilet and I asked for a commode, I was told there was no one available at the moment, and he would have to wait. Often they didn't come at all, or were so long in coming that one obviously couldn't contain one's self any longer.

Eddie became progressively frail and couldn't walk. Getting him in and out of a chair was a problem, and when he needed to use the toilet, he was often told that no one was available to help him, and that he would just have to wait as they were busy. Whatever you asked for, they were always busy. I wanted to wheel him into the garden for some air and I was always told there was no wheelchair available and no one was available to move him into the chair. He was nearly always cold, and nearly always sitting without pyjama bottoms with no one and nothing coming to take care of him. I felt hopeless and considered his position hopeless. At least on one occasion I managed to get help to get Eddie into a wheelchair to take him outside for a walk. Eddie escaped in the wheelchair down the ramp. He 'got away from the Germans', but nearly came a cropper when the chair almost tipped over. I said to him, 'You may have got away from the Germans, but you can't get away from me!'

I couldn't understand why Eddie was given very hot drinks for him to pick up and try to drink. It never registered on the staff that the drinks were very hot. If you complained you were treated with disdain. I was amazed to see them bring him a dirty dish with nothing but a spoonful of jelly or jam resting on it. I can only assume it was someone's leftover. Why bring him one spoonful of something in a dirty dish? It was brought by the same lady who had been so aggressive to me earlier on, and I felt I couldn't face another blast from her, especially as I worried about how they would treat Eddie when I was not there. In other words, they would take their annoyance with me out on him. It was a constant concern of mine.

At the time, Betty wrote:

I will not stand by any longer and see the appalling indignity my husband is suffering. If I don't get adequate help at once I'll alert the press, and ask: 'Is this the way to treat our war heroes?' There are days Eddie has suffered with his spine as a direct result of his landing in this country by parachute. I want him to die with dignity and I demand it for what he has done.

Fortunately, Eddie's last days were spent in a private, but state-funded, nursing home in Bricket Wood in St Albans. His companion in the home was Cliff Richard's mother. 'She was a bit batty and used to tell us how she needed to go and pick the children up from school. She just loved having tea and talking with Eddie.' But, Eddie being the ever-active Eddie, he had to sleep on a mattress on the floor as he kept falling out of bed and injuring himself. He was bedridden and often in pain, but Eddie's undying charisma could still hold an audience. 'He'd sit wearing a baseball cap, waiting for his friends to gather ... On other occasions, he would lie in bed, telling his stories.'[2]

'The last month of Eddie's life was emotional. A lot of thoughts went through Betty's mind such as: 'As you sow, so you shall reap'; 'nothing is achieved without inspiration'; 'be the person you want to become'. She says, 'I wanted to help my daughter have a good quality of life. I wanted to move away from my sad environment, and write a book about mine and Eddie's life; I wanted to get justice for the law suit, the loss of a million pounds.'

The last words spoken to me by Eddie I shall remember vividly forever, 'I love you', spoken to me whilst sitting on his bed in the nursing home a few days before he passed on. I was sitting up in the window and in my mind this was his farewell to me. I remember thinking this is the last thing I will hear from him. The same day I had discovered burns made on his body and was told by the nurse it was from thrashing about on the carpet during the night. I will never forget this feeling of desolation, how I was not there to help him through such a time of torment. I hate having to say that, but I need to. In fact, so many of Eddie's words will remain forever in my mind. Eddie's favourite quotes: 'I shall go but I shall always come back', and 'Never resist temptation'. (He never did!) And, with a smile, 'We've had 500 fights and I've never won one!' That is not really true; he still won the battles with me to the end. After all, if he could fool the German high command, he could easily fool me! When introducing me to anyone I had not met before he'd say, 'This is my wife Betty who has lived through six of my mistresses, haven't you darling?'

Betty has been heard to ask during this period, 'Where are your six mistresses now when I could do with them?'

Eddie died on 11 December 1997, the cause of death recorded as heart failure. As a measure of the affection in which Eddie was held, Princess Manijeh in Paris and Princess Shahnaz, the Shah of Iran's sister, were among the first to call when they heard of Eddie's death. Betty's friend Carol Bell also recalls the time, in which she remembers the consolation Betty received not just from royalty, but from hundreds of cards and letters from people all over the world, who had known them over the years. The newspaper obituaries recognised him as a very brave man, but many trotted out the old myths, uncorrected from years of accumulated clippings.

Betty didn't want a fuss, and so there was a private cremation attended only by close relatives:

We decided to have a very intimate funeral for Eddie with no outside people. The Wades were the only people other than family to attend; he was not only Eddie's doctor but a good friend. As we were leaving after the funeral, Tom Wade asked me to get out my pad and pen and start writing, so the only thing that I could assume was that he meant about Eddie's life.

That it would also be the story of her life didn't really occur to her.[3]

The distress from Eddie's injuries had become more severe as the years passed. He never received compensation for the damage to his back, though he did try for many years to get a pension. Eddie and Betty Chapman were both very annoyed and felt let-down when they saw less deserving cases awarded disability allowance. 'I can't understand it,' said the barrister Sir Lionel Thompson, who was in fine health, and one of their friends. 'I've been practising law since the war and I get a full disability allowance.'

Finally, a token gesture was made:

The year following Eddie's death, the Ministry of Defence rang up to ask if they could come to see me. I said yes, curious as to what the purpose was. One man came. The ministry had asked him to come and offer their condolences on the death of Eddie. We had tea and we chatted. He said that he didn't know Eddie but some people that he worked with that knew him talked of what a marvellous person he was, what great things he did and that he had great courage. As he was leaving, we shook hands and said goodbye. He put his hand in his pocket and pulled out an envelope in which was a cheque for £2,500. He said it was to help cover the bills. I was very touched at that moment, because this was the one and only time that anyone from this country had made any gesture towards his efforts. We lost so much, everything we ever did got ripped away, but my greatest loss was Eddie, who gambled his life for his country. I had a terrible fit of depression a few years after Eddie died, and I spent three months at University College Hospital. I don't remember much about it, but I had a very nice doctor who visited me as a friend as well.

Someone suggested that I do a whistle-stop journey of my life, saying it could be fascinating. The past is gone forever, a way of life that is not possible again. I needed to express my past in writing, otherwise my nieces and nephews and grandchildren would never know what my life has been. The process would also benefit me as a sort of therapy.

Betty's voice joins those of many others in honouring Eddie's life. Eddie was one of the few people ever to get a whole column by Walter Winchell,[4] a writer for the *New York Times*, and Eddie was one of the last to appear on *The Tonight Show Starring Johnny Carson* in New York, the number one show in America.

In general, the obituaries that appeared world-wide were complimentary about Eddie. Max Arthur, writing in *The Independent* newspaper on 6 January 1998, ended his thus:

Perhaps the greatest accolade for this extraordinary, complex and genial man who made an art-form of deception came from Baron Stefan von Gröning, the German Chapman had reported to while an agent. Although he had been deceived throughout the war, von Gröning attended the wedding of Eddie Chapman's daughter.

Even the German newspapers ran sympathetic obituaries, although they couldn't seem to help referring to Eddie as a 'Gentleman Gangster'.

Looking back, Betty remarks: 'The Germans didn't kill Eddie, but the loss of Shenley did.'

She also goes on to say: 'I believe I received a spirit message from Eddie after his death. On a visit to Queensberry Place in South Kensington, I visited a well-known medium who gave me a message from Eddie, which not only amazed me but made me happy. His message was: 'Tell her that there is a God.'

13

REFLECTIONS

In looking back over nine decades, Betty reflects:

My life has been enriched by so many people from all walks of life, of all colours, creeds and principles (and non-principles!). Africa in the 1950s was probably one of my most hair-raising experiences, but it was wonderful and very interesting. I often think that I have wasted my life. Yet looking back now at my life with Eddie, I cannot believe what I have done and accomplished. So instead of bemoaning a wasted life, I am putting that thought behind me and moving forward to happier thoughts, so that I can leave behind a more cheerful me. I made a commitment to have a child, but the intervening years have been very difficult, being mostly a one-parent family. I now reap the rewards. I have an extended family that brings me more joy than at any other time in my life.

So many people still make an effort to keep in touch, which means a lot to me. And I still meet new wonderful people very often, still today. Uzzi, the nephew of my taxi driver, gave me a note saying,

'The nation is waiting to hear from Betty Chapman, the wife of Zigzag; what's next?'

I think very fondly of a lot of people and I have quite a long string of people who keep in touch with me. I've made some good friends for life, I feel I really have. B. Graham, my assistant at Kilkea Castle kept in touch with me and wrote me poems until she died. Joan Carlisle was a very special lady and a very special friend to me. We met when we first got to Shenley. She was living in London with her husband and she gave us our twenty-fifth anniversary dinner, she cooked us beef wellington, which she prepared herself. She was a very famous opera singer at the time, singing in Covent Garden Opera House in London. She still calls me and says that she wants to visit, but not when she has to come to London for other reasons; she wants to come for me, and not share me with anything else. She is very special; she was convinced that Eddie saved us from the Germans.

My friend Carol Bell has taken a very active part whilst the books were being written over the past few years. It has taken her over a year to pick up Nick's book and read it for the second time. The first time she read it was just after it was published in 2007, and she was so full of it that she just couldn't take it all in.

Jane is the daughter of my very special friend, Stefanie Wareham. For me it was a happy day when I met Jane, who I have worked with over the past few months. We have achieved more in this short space of time (working on my own memoirs) than I achieved with Nicholas Booth who wrote *ZigZag*, which was the story of my husband's wartime work. Sadly for me, Jane has now left to live in Paris, which I know will not deter us from communicating. Jane is a very accomplished actress. It would make me so happy if she could become immortalised in my life, which she is helping to document. Barbara Cartland was an old, old friend of mine. [Betty has in her files a number of letters, notes and postcards from Barbara Cartland.] Everyone who was anyone knew Barbara.

The worst part of our life that I'd never want to relive was when we lost our first child, and it caused me to have deep depression that really lasted for some time. If I had to choose bits of my life to live again it would be the time in Iran, and the time in New York. I was in New York with Eddie. I loved the 21 Club in New York, as well as Central Park. We had a friend who lived on the East River in a famous block of flats and he was an enormously wealthy man who used to visit Eddie in Rome. I liked Rome too during the time I spent with Eddie there, that was a good time, but then it really depended how Eddie was behaving. If Eddie was having time out with other women it wasn't much fun, but if we were having a happy time together and sharing a good relationship, it was hilarious and a magical time.

People like Nicholas Booth have been a big part of the last few years of my life. The writing of the book was a huge thing. Nicholas and his agent Peter Cox came to see me sometimes; I even had a lovely birthday with them. When Ben Macintyre visited me I told him that I was working with Nicholas Booth on the story of Eddie and the war. I already had appointments in my diary for the dates I was meeting Nicholas, a sort of proof really. The book that Ben was writing was unauthorised as far as I was concerned. He has made lots of money from this book as well, of which of course I have not received one penny. *The Times* even published a story by Ben Macintyre, which claimed that von Gröning had deliberately set up Eddie as an assassin, when he offered to bring him into the presence of Adolf Hitler. I know that it was what von Gröning wanted; he had discussed it at length with Eddie, working out how he could kill him. Eddie never actually met Hitler, and thought it was an unworkable idea.

At the time of the work on *ZigZag* I heard news that George, von Gröning's son, who came to visit us with his dad at Shenley Lodge, had died. It was a terrible tragic death; he was killed by a falling tree. When he was over in England I tried to get George into a medical school here but I couldn't manage to help him. He studied in Germany and then started his own hospital in Bremen. He had hardly got to grips with that when his days came to an end. It was very saddening for me, he was very young, so I wrote a letter to his mother saying how sad I was and that Eddie was very attached to them and held them in a special place in his heart. He often talked of the times he spent with George's father. I wish to mention him in my book on our lives because he made such an impact, and von Gröning and Eddie were very fond of each other. He has since died, leaving only his wife and daughter. He used to tell me how Eddie saved his life (by demanding his recall from the Russian front). At a recent birthday I was at a restaurant with a lot of family and I really do remember sitting there thinking how far I have come, and how happy I was. I think it must have been my ninetieth birthday, and just as we were about to leave the band started playing and everyone sang happy birthday to me.

As noted earlier, Betty is a very spiritual person, and is a strong believer in reincarnation:

I've come back into this life because I believe in my last life I was wayward, never stayed anywhere very long, I was a drunkard, and I was irresponsible. Now this time, if you take my life, I've always been responsible for someone, first of all Eddie, and then our child, then for all of the places I have built and tried to build. I've stayed a long time in places – I had Shenley for thirty-one years. I hardly drink, just have the odd drink, and I've always been responsible for someone. It's redressing the balance in a way, I suppose.

I don't know what Eddie's was. I can't speak for him, but I regard him as my cross. It's karma, the redressing and rebalancing of ourselves that goes on over many lifetimes. This is the way I think, and this is the way I accept it.

There has been evidence in Betty's life to support this view. As previously mentioned, she received a message through a medium from Eddie after his passing. She also had another spirit message that she failed to recognise as such, but which lent credence to the veracity of Eddie's message:

One evening two young friends came to visit in Egerton Gardens. One of them was a young pilot called Bobby Ferguson and the other pilot was called Jeffrey Page of the Hadley-Page aviation family. They came to say goodbye because Bobby was going off to South America. We were talking about Geoffrey de Havilland because he had just been killed flying the Swallow. Shortly after this I was at a séance in London and a person came through identifying himself as Geoffrey and he said he had a person with him called Bobby who had been killed in uniform. Eddie and I discussed this, and he said that the only person that we knew called Bobby was Bobby Ferguson, but he was in South America. Some time after, on one of my return trips from Ghana, I was having lunch with a friend who looked across the restaurant at a young girl, and remarked, 'She'll be pretty when she grows up.' I turned to look at her and immediately recognised her as Bobby's daughter. I straight away went over to her and asked how her father was. She replied that he had been killed flying in South America. I was extremely shocked to hear this.

Unlike Betty, Eddie was never particularly religious. He used to say to me: 'Who knows the meaning of life? I'm damned if I do. We've been put on this Earth and we have all these quaint beliefs.' Eddie was fatalistic right up to the last. 'We are taught we are going to be responsible for all our sins,' he said. 'If so, I'll be on trial for the next hundred years!'

Betty is less than happy with the turn the world has taken in recent decades. When recalling her early life, she comments:

I know we were indeed very lucky despite our setbacks to have enjoyed such freedom from doom and gloom. Muggings and murderers hardly ever happened, and there was hardly any talk of terrorism. Television was very low-key, there were great films in the cinema, and wonderful theatre. Communications were perfectly adequate with no mobile phones or computers, and you counted on your fingers, not a calculator. Progress I feel has not bettered our life. Money-grabbing developers have ruined our country with money. I am happy I lived in the era I did, I simply loath life as it is today. In our days we had such good, clean fun and were able to walk in the streets and at all hours and anywhere, and go to bed without locking the doors and windows. Or, without being deafened with all the kind of noises of today – it cannot be called music. Everyone used to respect each other.

I was asked frequently how I managed to survive so many years with Eddie. When reflecting I am staggered, I think my religious background and my strong beliefs held me up throughout my long journey. I believe Eddie was moulded by his early life. His father was at sea a lot and he was usually left to his mother's attentions. He was very fond of his mother. He got a message one day to say that his mother was ill and could he go immediately. He went off to the hospital, a special one for people that had no money, called a 'poor house'. They were not nice places to die in. His mum saw him all dressed in his Guards uniform and was ever so proud of him. She died whilst he was there. Eddie grew very bitter; he was absolutely shocked and said that 'if that is the way that society would treat his mother then screw society!' His father was a marine engineer and always away at sea so his mother took care of all whilst he was growing up. Eddie's parents also had a pub called 'The Clipper Inn' in Sunderland. So Eddie went off to London; he bought an old bicycle and rode all the way there. Then when he got there he got mixed up with a bad gang of people and was going to nightclubs and started getting into trouble.

I was never sure if Eddie's experiences caused him to live in a wonderful fantasy on his own. In Norway he was facing certain execution for the slightest slip, and periods of solitary confinement also enabled him to live long periods alone. He spent two years in the Canaries with few past contacts. He also spent long periods at sea on the cargo boat. Another thing that stays in my mind is when his father died, and I said, 'Now you must go to the funeral.' He said, 'You come with me' but I said, 'No, you must go, it's your family.' Then he said, 'You are my family.' It took all my time to get him to go. He was always very hard about his father. Now whether it was because of the beatings, I don't know. They say that you knock one devil out and another devil comes in. He never seemed to want to have anything more to do with him.

Betty still fails to understand Eddie's treatment by the Security Service. She remembers when, many years later, the espionage writer Nigel West organised a reunion of the surviving wartime double agents, and Eddie was deliberately not invited. Eventually, at West's insistence, a number of wartime case officers very grudgingly allowed Eddie to attend.

Betty sees this as a result of Eddie's 'not being one of us' in the eyes of the Security Services. Her opinion is that the Security Services were always pretty impressed with themselves, and Eddie made them look foolish. 'Any way they could undermine him, they would,' Betty states. 'The problem was MI5 didn't like any criticism.' And though the service maintained that Eddie had been remunerated handsomely – mostly by the Germans (which they fail to note) – Betty remarks that they 'weren't so generous once they had finished using him'.

Betty is not happy with the way Eddie has been portrayed in the media. Remarking about the portrayal of him in a television documentary, she says:

His voice was spoken by an actor who spoke with a very harsh East End of London accent. It sounded nothing like Eddie, who spoke with a very cultured accent. And when his MI5 files were released, all the press commented on was his criminal past and his womanising. It always made me laugh when Eddie was described as a 'master safe-cracker'. If you ever got locked out, Eddie could never pick a lock and get you in. He might have been able to take a crowbar to it. He was the most useless man in the house. That is probably why they used gelignite!

Betty remarks with some force:

Eddie was paid by the Germans but never by the British; why give Eddie a bouquet with one hand and stick a knife in his back with another? He was treated so badly. I frequently became outraged at the character assassination of Eddie, which just seemed to go on and on. Perhaps I am wrong with my attitude, but I cannot forgive whoever was responsible for the grief inflicted on Eddie throughout his life after the war until he died. So, in the end, the Germans were paying for his day-to-day existence. Conspiracy was rife, not by the press but by our own people, so I was always careful who I spoke to and what I said. But the CIA and the FBI came to visit Eddie in London once the war was over to say how grateful they were to him, as his work also helped the Americans. I recently came across a note in Eddie's war records saying that he had been suggested for a decoration. Many people have since said that they will fight to get him the acknowledgement that he deserved but no one has kept their word.

Eddie was philosophical about his lack of official recognition. He told Frank Owen: 'My luck with those fellows (the Security Services) is wearing thin. I'm not collecting gongs [medals], and anyway, I have my Iron Cross.' But sadly, in his last months and looking back, Eddie remarked: 'They didn't even say thank you.'

Betty says quietly:

I wonder, if he was alive today, how Eddie would enjoy the current political circumstances. Also, what he would think about all those who are still going on about him. I wonder if he would still deny so many things and still be as interesting to people. Eddie always had a capacity for turning tables, I wonder if it would still be the same. He was very popular wherever he went. I was there at the beginning of his fame, and I found it difficult. He was always strong like a rock. You could understand that he could do what he did.

Betty doesn't always recognise the part she played in Eddie's life. Lilian Verner-Bonds remarks:

For all of his life he had Betty there. Even during his time in Germany he still knew that she was there. I remember that every time I spoke to Eddie, it was always Betty this and Betty that. She was always at the front of his life. I remember coming to Shenley and walking around with Eddie. He would always be saying, 'Where's Betty?'

Because of Lilian's long-time friendship with the Chapmans, and as a keen observer of humanity, she has the last word about Betty's life with Eddie: 'She was the anchor of his life. She was the core and the rock.'

NOTES

Prologue

1. *The Guardian*, Wednesday 24 January 2007.

Chapter 1

1. In the Church of England, also called the Anglican Church, the ordained minister of a local congregation is called a vicar, from the Latin *vicarius*. In other Christian denominations he would be called the minister or the priest.

Chapter 2

1. The International Isle of Man TT (Tourist Trophy) Race is a motorcycle-racing event held on the island. In the 1930s, the TT

races became the predominant international motor-cycling event in the racing calendar, and the decade is seen as the classic era of racing in the Isle of Man.

2. Betty is referring to Mayfair SW1, one of the most exclusive areas in London.

3. The British Security Service, commonly known as MI5 (Military Intelligence, Section 5) is the United Kingdom's counter-intelligence and security agency and is part of the intelligence machinery alongside the Secret Intelligence Service (SIS, or MI6).

4. In civilian life Jasper Maskelyne was an accomplished magician and illusionist. They covered the entire roof of the powerhouse with canvas and painted it to look as if it had been sabotaged. They made papier mâché dummies of pieces of the sabotaged generator and added chipped chunks of brick and cracked cement blocks etc., in order to fool the surveillance aircraft that were allowed to fly over the scene.

5. The highly decorated Group Captain (Colonel) John 'Cat's Eyes' Cunningham (1917–2002), was a Royal Air Force night-fighter ace during the Second World War and a test pilot, both before and after the war. He was credited with twenty kills, of which nineteen were claimed at night. Cunningham returned to de Havilland as a test pilot after the war. In 1946, he succeeded Betty's friend Geoffrey de Havilland as chief test pilot following the latter's death. He went on to test the de Havilland Comet, the world's first jet airliner.

6. This book was later turned into a film of the same name, starring Dirk Bogarde.

7. Also called 'doodlebugs' and 'buzz bombs' by the British. Betty uses the term 'buzz bombs' in her recollections of the time.

8. Squares have long been a feature of London. A few were built as public open spaces, but most of them originally contained private communal gardens for use by the inhabitants of the surrounding houses.

9. Sir Archibald McIndoe (1900–60) was a pioneering New Zealand plastic surgeon who worked for the RAF during the Second World War. He greatly improved the treatment and rehabilitation of badly burned aircrew, and received a knighthood in 1947 for his innovative work and reconstructive surgery techniques.

Chapter 3

1. His father was Air Chief Marshal Sir Keith Park. He was in operational command during the Battle of Britain and later in the Battle of Malta. In February 1945 he was appointed Allied Air Commander, South East Asia.

2. Kensington is a district of west and central London. The area has some of London's most expensive streets and squares.

3. Dame Elizabeth Rosemond 'Liz' Taylor, DBE was a British-American actress. She appeared in her first motion picture at the age of 9, and became one of the all-time great Hollywood screen actresses. Her much-publicised personal life included eight marriages. From the mid-1980s, she championed HIV and AIDS programmes, and received numerous awards and honours for her charity work.

4. George Burns was an American comedian, actor and writer, whose career successfully spanned vaudeville, film, radio and television. A television pioneer, he is probably remembered best for taking his successful radio programme *The Burns and Allen Show* to television in 1950. Burns was also a best-selling author who wrote a total of ten books. One of his most famous lines was: 'When I was young, they called me a rebel. When I was middle-aged, they called me eccentric. Now that I'm old, I'm doing the same thing I've always done and they call me senile.' He died in 1996, at the age of 100.

5. One of London's premier restaurants of the time.

6. Another wealthy London enclave.

7. Kathleen Ryan was born in Dublin of Tipperary parentage and was a spirited and heart-warming actress who appeared in British and Hollywood movies between 1947 and 1957. She was one of Ireland's great beauties of her time, and a long-time friend of the Chapmans.

8. James Neville Mason was an English actor who attained stardom in both British and American films. Mason remained a powerful figure in the industry throughout his career and was nominated for three Academy Awards as well as three Golden Globes.

9. The Rothschild family is a European dynasty of German-Jewish origin that established European banking and finance houses starting in the late eighteenth century. The British branch of the family was elevated to British nobility at the request of Queen Victoria. The name of Rothschild became synonymous with extravagance and great wealth. The dynasty was also renowned for its art collecting, its palaces and its philanthropy.

Chapter 4

1. The hustle and bustle of this traditional Devon shipbuilding and fishing village appealed to Eddie after his brother became a director of Appledore Shipyard. Eddie eventually bought a house in Odun Road.
2. The Troubles: the insurrection against British rule.
3. The Irish Republican Army was a paramilitary organisation seeking the end of British rule in Northern Ireland and the unification of the province with the Republic of Ireland. In 2005 the IRA announced an end to its armed campaign.
4. Quoted in *ZigZag*, by Nicholas Booth.
5. Stormont was the location of the Northern Ireland government of the day.
6. Aristotle Onassis was a Greek shipping magnate who developed a huge fleet of supertankers and freighters. His second marriage was to Jacqueline Bouvier Kennedy, the widow of US President John F. Kennedy, in 1968.
7. Maria Callas was an American operatic soprano, whose much-publicised volatile temperament resulted in numerous lengthy feuds with rivals and managers. She had a long and intimate relationship with Onassis prior to his marriage to Jacqueline Kennedy.
8. Richard Burton, CBE was a Welsh actor nominated seven times for an Academy Award, and at one time was the highest-paid actor in Hollywood. He is most remembered in the public consciousness for his turbulent marriages to his second wife, actress Elizabeth Taylor.

9. Paul Douglas (1907–59) was an American actor, who began his career as a stage actor. He began appearing in films in 1949.

10. Audrey Hepburn (1929–93) was a British actress and humanitarian. She became one of the most successful film actresses in the world and performed with notable leading men. She starred as Eliza Doolittle in the film version of *My Fair Lady* (1964), becoming only the third actor to receive US $1,000,000 for a film role. By the mid-1950s, she was not only one of the biggest motion picture stars in Hollywood, but also a major fashion icon.

11. Burl Ivanhoe Ives (1909–95) was an American actor, writer and folk-music singer. As an actor, Ives's work included comedy, drama and voice work in theatre, television and motion pictures.

Chapter 5

1. Easily equivalent to ten times or more that amount today.
2. Belgravia is a district of central London in the City of Westminster, lying to the south-west of Buckingham Palace. Noted for its immensely expensive residential properties, it is one of the wealthiest districts in the world.
3. Krobo Edusei was a high-profile member of Kwame Nkrumah's government. He was a popular, outspoken and prominent Ashanti activist and at the forefront of the Ghanaian independence movement, galvanising support amongst the Ashantis for Nkrumah's independence movement. He served as Minister without Portfolio, Minister for Transport and Communication, and Minister for the Interior, under Nkrumah.

Chapter 6

1. Because of the primitive telephone system in Ghana, most communication was by short-wave radio.

2. A British term for Native Americans, used to distinguish them from natives of India.
3. The Golden Stool is the royal and divine throne of the Ashanti people. Such seats were traditionally symbolic of a chieftain's leadership, but the Golden Stool is believed to house the spirit of the Ashanti nation – living, dead and yet to be born. And, female. Eddie is mistaken about its construction. It is wood overlaid with gold.
4. Squadron Leader Guy Gibson, VC was the leader of the famous 'dambusters' squadron.
5. Sir Lionel Thompson, CBE was Deputy Master and Controller of the Royal Mint from 1950–57.

Chapter 7

1. *The Red Beret* was retitled *Paratrooper* for its US release, and is a fictitious story about an American who enlists in the British Parachute Regiment (wearers of the Red Beret) in 1940, claiming to be a Canadian. The film starred the American actor Alan Ladd.
2. Albert Romolo 'Cubby' Broccoli (1909–96), was an American film producer who made more than forty motion pictures. Broccoli followed Terence Young as the producer, along with Harry Saltzman, of the later James Bond films.
3. Soho in London's West End. For much of the twentieth century Soho had a seamy reputation for sex shops as well as nightlife and film industry. Since its transformation in the 1980s, the area is now predominantly a fashionable district of upmarket restaurants and media offices.
4. Barbara Woolworth Hutton (1912–79) was the heiress to the retail tycoon Frank W. Woolworth. Seven times married, she was often dubbed 'Poor Little Rich Girl' because of her troubled life. Her life made great media copy and she was roundly exploited by them. She committed suicide in 1979.
5. Sir Reginald Carey 'Rex' Harrison (1908–90) was an English actor of stage and screen. One of Harrison's best remembered film roles

was that of Professor Henry Higgins in the stage and film versions of *My Fair Lady*.

6. Kay Kendall (1927–59) was an English actress. She began a romantic relationship with actor Rex Harrison after they appeared together in the comedy film *The Constant Husband* (1955), and they were married in 1957.

7. At that time Morocco was a French protectorate, and the Sultan was in exile in Madagascar. Moroccan nationalism was beginning to strongly assert itself, and the Sultan's return would have had serious consequences for the French. Independence from France was attained in 1956.

Chapter 8

1. Yul Brynner, *Yuliy Borisovich Briner* (1920–85) was a Russian-born actor, best known for his portrayal of the King of Siam in the musical *The King and I*. His other well-known role was as Chris in *The Magnificent Seven*. He was noted for his distinctive voice and for his shaven head, his personal trademark.

2. Romy Schneider (1938–82) was an Austrian-born German film actress who also held French citizenship. She made sixty films and was the recipient of many awards. The French film industry initiated the Prix Romy Schneider (Romy Schneider Award), the most prestigious award for promising upcoming actresses.

3. Claudine Auger (born Claudine Oger on 26 April 1941) is a French actress best known for her role as Bond girl Dominique 'Domino' Derval in the James Bond film *Thunderball* (1965). She earned the title of Miss France Monde and was also the first runner-up in the 1958 Miss World contest.

Chapter 9

1. Lilian Verner-Bonds is a noted author and colour-therapist, and long-time friend of the Chapmans.

2. Elstree Studios is a generic term that can refer to several film studios based in or around the towns of Borehamwood and Elstree in Hertfordshire, England. A number of studios have existed in this area since film production began in the late 1920s. They are all owned by different organisations and produce both motion pictures and television programmes. MGM was among the more prominent of them.

3. Patrick Wymark (1926–70) was a British, stage, film and television actor. He took his acting name from his grandfather-in-law, the writer William Wymark Jacobs. He had four children, one being the actress Jane Wymark.

4. John Conteh (b. 1951) was world light-heavyweight boxing champion, and one of Britain's most successful boxers. He was considered good enough to be an opponent of Muhammad Ali, although this never came about.

5. Lady Henrietta Guinness of the famous brewing family, jumped off a bridge at Spoleto – the ancient cultural city in Umbria, Italy – in 1978, at the age of 35. She said once: 'If I had been poor, I would have been happy.'

6. The Profumo Affair was a 1963 British political scandal named after John Profumo, Secretary of State for War. His affair with Christine Keeler, the reputed mistress of an alleged Russian spy, followed by lying in the House of Commons when he was questioned about it, forced the resignation of Profumo and damaged the reputation of Prime Minister Harold Macmillan's government. Macmillan himself resigned a few months later due to 'ill health'.

7. Reported in: www.spartacus.schoolnet.co.uk

8. This is according to Betty; the 'official' version is different.

9. Harley Street in London is the location of a large number of medical practices, and is synonymous with it. When a Londoner speaks of 'Harley Street' it is automatically assumed that medical matters are being referred to. It is a significant distance from Shenley Lodge, and would have involved a great deal of travelling for Betty.

Chapter 10

1. Franklin Roy 'Frank' Bruno MBE (b. 16 November 1961) is an English former boxer, who won the WBC heavyweight championship in 1995. He has remained a popular celebrity with the British public since his ring career ended, and appears regularly as an actor in Christmas pantomimes.

2. This was a time in Britain and Ireland when women in top executive positions were extremely rare, and generally much resented by male executives.

3. Tithing, (from Old English *teogothian*, 'tenth'), is an ancient custom adopted by the Christian Church whereby lay people contributed one-tenth of their income either in money, goods, or produce, for religious purposes, and often under legal or ecclesiastical compulsion. It was abolished in Ireland in 1871. A tithe table lists all things tithable, and the times at which certain tithes are due.

4. Sir John Mills (1908–2005) was an English actor who made more than 120 films in a career spanning seven decades. From 1959 through the mid-1960s, Mills starred in several films alongside his daughter Hayley.

5. Dame Mary Barbara Hamilton Cartland (1901-2000) was an English author, one of the most prolific of the twentieth century. She was one of London's most prominent society figures and one of Britain's most popular media personalities, appearing often at public events and on television, speaking on issues such as love, health, and social and political issues.

Chapter 11

1. Mohammad Rezā Shāh (1919–80) was the last Shah of Iran, who ruled Iran from September 1941 until his overthrow by the Iranian Revolution in 1979. The Shah's White Revolution, intended to transform Iran into a global power, succeeded in modernising the

nation, nationalising many natural resources, and extending suffrage to women. His modernisation of Iran and his pro-Western stance set him at odds with Muslim fundamentalists.

2. Princess Basma bint Talal of Jordan is the sister of the late King Hussein of Jordan and paternal aunt to the current king of Jordan, King Abdullah II. She is considered to be the Princess Royal of Jordan.

3. Princess Shahnaz Pahlavi (b. 27 October 1940) is the first child of the late Shah of Iran and his first wife, Princess Fawzia of Egypt.

4. Qom is considered a holy city by Shi'a Islam, being the site of the shrine of Fatema Mæ'sume, sister of Imam 'Ali ibn Musa Rida (Persian *Imam Reza*, 789–816 AD). It is the largest centre for Shi'a scholarship in the world, and is a major destination of pilgrimage.

5. The name comes from the shape of a throne, having the figures of two peacocks standing behind it, their tails being expanded and the whole of the throne inlaid with sapphires, rubies, emeralds, pearls and other precious stones.

Chapter 12

1. 'School celebrations make investor "sick"', *The Times*, article by Emma Schrimsley.

2. Quoted in *ZigZag*, by Nicholas Booth.

3. And, of course, it is the source of much of the material in this book.

4. Walter Winchell (1897–1972) was an American newspaper and radio gossip commentator. Although controversial among his broadcast colleagues, he was one of the most listened to men in America.

Chapter 13

1. This was written in 2008.

ACKNOWLEDGEMENTS

Thanks to the Chapman family, and especially to Betty's daughter, for the use of documents, tapes, photographs and other materials relating to the life of this extraordinary woman. Thanks also to The History Press, and especially to Mark Beynon, and to Nigel West for his foreword.

INDEX

Visit our website and discover thousands of other History Press books.
www.thehistorypress.co.uk